Beating Art[ ] Alternative Cooking

Baker Dan

Photographer: Mira Blushtein

Editor: Elinoar Rabin

Includes: Nutrition Facts

Gluten-Free

Baker Dan LLC

Published by Baker Dan, LLC., New York, NY.

ISBN: 978-0-9894380-1-8 (pbk.)

Publisher's Cataloging-in-Publication Data

Baker Dan.

Beating arthritis: alternative cooking / Baker Dan.

pages cm

ISBN: 978-0-9894380-1-8 (pbk.)

ISBN: 978-0-9894380-2-5 (e-book)

Includes bibliographical references and index.

1. Inflammation—Diet therapy—Recipes. 2. Gluten-free diet—Recipes. 3. Sugar-free diet—Recipes. 4. Milk-free diet—Recipes. 5. Self-care, Health.   I. Title.

RB131 .B35 2013

641.5`6318—dc23

2013919239

Manufactured in the United States of America

With deep appreciation and gratitude, to Chayah and Gilad, my culinary arts teachers.

Acknowledgments

This book would not have been written without the warm support of my colleagues, friends and family. The list that follows is long, but if I left anyone out, I apologize.

First and foremost is my dear friend Elinoar Rabin, who has accompanied me on my culinary journey from the very beginning many years ago, when I was still studying to become a chef. A life-long editor, food journalist, cookbook author, and publisher, Elinoar has followed this book from its inception to completion. It is Elinoar's stewardship that has given this book its form and made it more accessible and user-friendly for the reader.

My linguistic editor, August Tarrier, meticulously combed the book and greatly improved its readability and user-friendliness. August opened my eyes to the blind spots in the recipes, weeded out the mistakes and omissions, and made the recipes easier to follow and enjoy.

A cook book comes alive with its photos. I look at a good food photo and start salivating before even reading the recipes. The beautiful photos in this book were taken by my friend Mira Blushtein, a fashion photographer by training and a passionate people's photographer. It is always a pleasure to work with Mira, and it is her patience, appreciation for the smallest details, and good spirit that has made the photos in this book the wonders that they are.

Writing this book turned out to be a much longer journey than I had envisioned. That may be because I found it difficult to frame the personal story behind the recipes. I am grateful to Susan and David Matzner, my dear cousins and friends, who opened their hearts and their home in upstate New York to me, which allowed me to write draft after draft in the most peaceful and beautiful environment possible.

My children, Adam, Ori and Roni were the most effective task-masters in that they continuously monitored the progress of the book. I could fool myself and the adult world with the usual adult excuses, but children live by different rules, and this book was no exception. Thank you, guys; without you, I might not have been ready to publish until I was a grandpa.

To my wife, Tal: your patience with me is one of life's mysteries, and as I regard love, I do not want to delve too deep – because, it is best to leave some beautiful riddles untouched.

Table of Contents

INTRODUCTION

This book grapples with a basic question: How do you handle food restrictions? Suppose you had been eating pretty much whatever you wanted, and then, because of a health issue, or because you simply wanted to feel better, many foods that you once enjoyed are no longer "allowed." My stance is: Don't panic, you can still enjoy a varied and versatile diet even if you're restricting certain foods.

Beating Arthritis shows you a method of how to prevent and reduce the inflammation of chronic disease and an attitude of never giving up. It is not a magic cure, but instead a way of eating, one that will pay off if you persevere. "Alternative Cooking" suggests an alternative approach to cooking and an alternative way of using ingredients.

In this book you will find answers for many of your questions. What if you cannot eat certain fruits and vegetables, even when you are a vegetarian or a vegan? What if you need to eliminate wheat flour, added sugar or fats, or certain spices? If you're gluten-free, dairy-free, sugar-free, or fat-free, can you still make tasty, appealing and nutritious meals? Of course you can.

Seventeen years ago, when I was in my early forties, I was diagnosed with Palindromic Rheumatoid Arthritis (PRA). My wife, Tal, and I were living on Central Park West in Manhattan in a well-lighted one-bedroom apartment. I was busy working on my field research for my doctorate in education, observing and video-recording young children and their male teachers as they interacted during the day. The previous year I had fulfilled my childhood dream by finishing my flight training and becoming a private pilot. I was also busy playing my electric guitar, writing songs and putting together a demo CD. Tal was working as an analyst in an investment company, and traveling the world visiting food companies, her specialty. Our first son was had not yet been born, although we had already started planning for a child.

9

My first signs of Palindromic Rheumatoid Arthritis (PRA) were redness on the side of my right index finger at the middle joint. At first I didn't pay it any mind, although it was a bit red and warm, but then the joint began to swell, until eventually the finger had nearly doubled in size and was very painful. I began a lengthy medical odyssey, going to a variety of Western, Chinese, and Alternative doctors, and I eventually changed my diet. People often ask me to explain how I dealt with PRA through diet, and this book is a summary of what I have learned.

The book has been written from a patient's point of view, not from a medical one. Formally, I have two professions. I became a pastry chef in Israel, graduating in 1989 from The Central Hotel Training School, named after Aryeh Avisar, located at the "Tadmor" Hotel, Herzliya, Israel. I am also a professional educator, having earned a Ph.D. in Education from New York University in 2003, a Master of Science in Education (MSE) from Bank Street College of Education in 1991, and a BA in Education and English Literature from the Hebrew University in 1983.

The recipes in the book include detailed Nutrition Facts. In the nutritional analysis I have used the term "portion" instead of "serving." The food industry uses the FDA term "serving" on food labels, and this term indicates a legal range of weights that is ascribed to each particular food. The FDA publishes the guidelines for Serving Size under a "Food Labeling Guide" that appears on the FDA website. The term "portion" makes more sense in the realm of home cooking, as it is an estimate, according to pragmatic experience, of the number of people who can enjoy a particular recipe.

In one section, Side Dishes, I did not include Nutrition Facts. These are essentially one ingredient dishes and in this section my intent was to demonstrate how to prepare these dishes. Nutrition Facts for single ingredients can be found in "National Nutrient Database for Standard Reference" published by the United States Department of Agriculture (http://ndb.nal.usda.gov/ndb/search/list#http://ndb.nal.usda.gov/ndb/search/list).

The recipes are all gluten-free, lactose-free, with no added sugar or fat, and all are Kosher. While I have included vegetarian recipes, I have also included recipes for fish, poultry, and beef.

After my diagnosis, I was confronted with the unknown; it took me a long while to slough off the awkward sense that I was alone in this enterprise of retooling what I ate and how I prepared my meals. Writing this book has been a cathartic experience for me: I have had to cope with a whole new set of unexpected demands, and the book has helped me to peel off the layers of the long journey. My message to the reader is simple: Write, share. Please do not feel alone in your struggle, because you are not the first or the last to be confronted with profound changes in your health. Please send your comments and questions to dan@bakerdan.com, or visit my website at www.bakerdan.com.

The Essence of Alternative Cooking

Alternative cooking (and alternative baking) is in essence a process of elimination: Fewer ingredients rather than more. Simplicity instead of complexity: eat fewer calories, eliminate processed food, and make your own food with your own hands. There is no cure for arthritis in its numerous forms, but for some, preventative measures, such as controlling one's diet, works. The medical world is divided on this point, and I have found two major camps: one camp says that diet has no effect on arthritis, and the other says it does make a difference. For example, Drs. Harry Spiera, Leslie D. Kerr, and Ts'ai-fan Yu belong to the former camp, while Dr. Grant Cooper belongs to the latter (see Bibliography at the end of the book).

I believe that the book is applicable to people suffering from other illnesses beside PRA, for example diabetes, or celiac disease. I have put "Arthritis" in the title because of my personal history, but the method I am describing in this book of changing one's eating habits can apply to coping with the dietary restrictions of other illnesses as well.

The idea behind alternative cooking is simple: cut the suspect list. For example, if you are dealing with arthritis in one of its many forms, you want to identify the causes that are under your control, and avoid or at least reduce or inflammation. Inflammation is often treated with medication and the problem with anti-inflammatory medications is that they often have side effects; some of them are well-known and accepted, and some are particular to the individual who takes the anti-inflammatories. I took various anti-inflammatory medications over the years that included steroids and non-steroids anti-inflammatory medications (NSAIDs). Altogether, I experienced the following side effects: Insomnia, anxiety, restlessness, aggression, stomachache, muscle-loss, weight-loss, memory-loss and creativity-loss.

The brain fog and confusion that one may experience from anti-inflammatory medications can make it especially difficult to undertake a new regimen or effect sustained change. There is no question that habits are difficult to break, but beginning an alternative cooking regimen can lower or free you from reliance on medication and allow you to rely instead on simplicity and rolling up your sleeves.

If you check out my recipes for fish, chicken and beef, you'll see that they're the essence of simplicity. If we focus primarily on taste for a moment, then in fact these ingredients come ready made. The grass that the cow grazed on provides flavor and ensures that the meat will be tasty. The same goes for chicken and fish—their habitats provide all they need. Adding spices to beef is like adding sugar to tea or coffee: who needs it? The sugar masks the wonderful natural taste inherent in the coffee or tea.

I mainly use stock to enhance the taste of fish, beef and chicken. Before I prepare the dish I make sure that I have enough fish stock, beef stock or chicken stock on hand. In the recipes you will find few additional ingredients to complement the taste, but the core is simple: the beef, chicken or fish by themselves. And sometimes you don't even need stock. The fat that is already in the meat will give it a wonderful taste.

The major goal in alternative cooking is quite basic: Food is primary, gratification is secondary. If an ingredient causes you inflammation, it is out of the picture: Plain, simple, and effective. The choice is stark: A full belly and a clear mind or a bursting belt and brain fog. At the heart of alternative cooking are the essentials of good nutrition: keep them balanced and they will provide the foundation. In the next section I detail the simple available tools that give us the basic nutritional information we need.

Understanding Good Nutrition

Luckily, the basics of good nutrition are very well presented and explained by three respected and easily accessible United States Department of Agriculture sources: *Choose MyPlate* (http://www.choosemyplate.gov), *Dietary Guidelines for Americans 2010* (http://www.health.gov/dietaryguidelines/dga2010/DietaryGuidelines2010.pdf), and *National Nutrient Database for Standard Reference* (http://ndb.nal.usda.gov/ndb/search/list#http://ndb.nal.usda.gov/ndb/search/list).

The titles are easy to find via a web search, but the addresses tend to change (the ones above were accurate in 2013 when we went to press). *Choose MyPlate* replaced a previous tool called *The Food Pyramid* and includes five Food Groups:

Vegetables, Fruits, Grains, Dairy products and Protein. The *Dietary Guidelines for Americans 2010* is a treasure trove of nutritional information that explains how to choose from these five groups to achieve a balanced d0iet, stay fit, and prevent obesity. This is a wonderful source of information that is right there, free of charge, on the web. You can either view it or download and print it, and you have a great, detailed nutritional and exercise guide. The guidelines are updated, by law, every five years.

The USDA's *National Nutrient Database for Standard Reference* provides nutritional facts for numerous foods. It is a standard reference, but not all commercial foods are listed. For those that did not show up in the Database, I provided nutritional facts directly from the package. For this book I used the *nutraCoster Professional* (version 2.1, revision 01/25/2011) nutritional software, which provides basic nutritional data based on the *National Nutrient Database for Standard Reference*.

You will notice that with all the recipes in this book, I have employed substitutions. For example, I do not include any dairy, but I have used soy milk instead (fortified soy milk contains the calcium that you need from dairy products). All the recipes are gluten-free as well, but we do include corn and brown rice.

Just a word about supplements: if you eat a balanced diet, you will have all the nutrients you need, without having to resort to supplements. The only reason to take a supplement would be if you had eliminated a certain food and could only get a necessary nutrient via the supplement.

Self-Study and the Safe List

What should you eat and what should you avoid eating in order to manage your arthritis? Please do not begin this journey on your own; at a minimum, consult your personal physician and a registered dietician.

The path to compiling a Safe List of ingredients and to creating a balanced diet includes four steps.

STEP ONE: Have a medical checkup to make sure you are getting all the necessary nutrients.

STEP TWO: During a week when you have some downtime, and guided by either your personal physician or a registered dietician, try a cleansing diet. Be patient and consider keeping a journal to record your sensations and responses. Keep it simple—a sentence or two will suffice. Of course, if you have an epiphany during your four-day fruit-and-vegetable-fast and you find yourself embarking on a rebuttal to *The Canterbury Tales*, go for it!

STEP THREE: Assisted by your medical team, gradually re-introduce foods to your diet. You'll need to be rigorous about this process: Add one ingredient at a time, and allow between 24 and 48 hours to gauge your response. Not all ingredients trigger responses in the same time interval.

Note your responses in your journal. You have a dual purpose here: by logging your responses, you are building your own database of what to eat and to avoid, and you are also providing your physician with a log of your inflammation occurrences.

As I have mentioned, arthritis still does not have a cure, but it is important to keep in mind that you can make a substantial difference in how you feel; it is likely that if you keep at it, you will have less inflammation and better nutritional habits. You may be able to reduce or even eliminate your need for medication. If you do have occasional outbreaks of arthritis and need to take medicine, note your responses, both physical and mental, in your journal. Bring your notes to your personal physician and consult about whether to stay on the same medication or switch to another.

In the final analysis, when it comes to your body and soul, you are more knowledgeable than anyone else. You have the most intimate knowledge and you are the final arbiter. We are not going for the "aha" moment when you suddenly realize one day that you are completely cured; rather, the payoff is that you will be much better informed about how to fight your own arthritis on a daily basis and in a way that is least disruptive to your life.

You are in charge of not only what to eat and what to avoid, but also of what medications to take in various situations. No physician can tell you how your body and soul will react to a specific medication (or, for that matter, what your reaction to a certain food will be). The insert that comes with your medication may not include your particular side effects, and that is because your response may be different from the one most commonly experienced.

You may have read articles that claim a certain ingredient or additive can heal arthritis. I suggest that you treat these ingredients or additives the way you would any other food that you want to add, namely, one at a time (and, of course, be sure to consult with your personal physician or registered dietician).

I would be especially careful with additives, for two reasons. First, I believe that a balanced diet has all the nutrients we need. Second, one of the major tenets of my approach is to control the ingredients. When you take additives, you do not actually know what else they may contain; those other materials could be the culprits. If you do decide to take additives, do it under medical supervision. If these additives are over-the-counter, check the ingredients. The same additive might be manufactured in different forms and made with different ingredients. Or one brand's manufacturing process might be slightly different than another. You might be surprised to learn that your body could respond differently to the same additive made by two different manufacturers.

I do not recommend any one ingredient or additive simply because each person is different and there are many kinds of arthritis. My intention with *Beating Arthritis* is twofold: I want to provide a detailed method of medically guided self-study for compiling a Safe List of Ingredients. And I want to help you use that Safe List to prepare tasty and varied recipes.

STEP FOUR: Finalize your Safe List and stick to it. After a while you will know exactly what works for you—what ingredients are good for you, at what time of the day, and in what quantities. You will also know what medications are the most suitable for you with the fewest side effects. Armed with this knowledge, sit down and summarize your Safe List of ingredients. One easy way to think about the list is by going over your day. Ask yourself: What do I eat for breakfast, lunch and dinner? Write down the menus, break them down into various ingredients and organize the ingredients according to the food categories: Fruits, Vegetables, Grains, etc. (for an example, see Appendix: Dan's Safe List).

After you have put together your Safe List, stick to it! This is a crucial point. Be wary of allowing yourself lapses or adding ingredients here and there, telling yourself, "I'll try this and, worst case scenario, I'll up my medication dose." In the moment, it is easy to tell yourself that eating a favorite food would not matter, but in the long run you run the risk of both increasing your inflammation and of losing sight of your goal.

Adhering to the Safe List is particularly challenging when you travel. My unequivocal advice to you: Bring or make your own food! It's true that this will require some planning, but you will save yourself a lot of trouble and agony of having to resort to medication. Besides, how nice to have your own home-cooked meals and to rest in the knowledge that you chose to be independent, creative and healthy in any environment.

Variety in Cooking

Choosing to restrict your food choices means that you will need to be especially creative in your approach to cooking in order to make sure you maintain variety. There are three major ways to create variety and they are usually combined, allowing you maximum leverage with the same ingredients (in Suggested Reading, at the end of the book, I added several excellent method books that explain the following in much greater detail).

The first way is to cook the ingredients differently. One major part of this method is connected to what I regard as the *biggest secret in cooking and baking*: *The ratio of solids to liquids*. For example, the difference between crunchy chocolate chip cookies and chewy ones is that the former stay in the oven five minutes longer and the recipe includes less liquid. It is easy to see how they end up crunchier. But you have to have some liquid—otherwise, you had just have burnt food. Fast, simple and unforgiving, as anyone who has ever cooked or baked can attest.

Think about the difference between rare, medium, and well done steaks. It all comes down to the amount of liquid in the steak and the attentiveness of the grill master. A lot of liquid and you have a rare steak. No liquids at all: the steak is over and so is your date.

The different cooking techniques, such as boiling, baking, grilling, frying and searing, all differ in the way that heat is applied to the ingredients, and that affects the outcome. In this book you will find, for example, that yams and sweet potatoes can be baked into chips, cooked in water or seared in a pan.

A second way to create variety is to mechanically treat the ingredient in different ways. Let me use the simplest example of making a fruit dessert. You can serve whole fruit, you can peel it, chop it coarsely, or finely, mash it, or run it through a blender. In each instance you'll get a different dessert—the texture and even the smell will differ.

A third way is to combine the ingredients with other ingredients. In the Side Dishes chapter, ingredients are prepared and served by themselves. Corn can be delicious served simply on the cob, but the very same corn, when its kernels are combined in a dish, will look and taste different. It is worth mentioning that corn is also available in several forms as a grain: coarse corn meal, medium corn meal, polenta, fine corn meal or corn flour. All of these different forms have different uses, resulting in a variety of tastes and textures.

A Word about Measurements

The measurements in this book are precisely calibrated and are made in weights for solids, and volume (and weight) for liquids. I provided both Imperial and Metric units, ounces and grams, cups and liters. There are few reasons for this approach. It is not really accurate to measure by volume (one cup of lettuce), or by unit (three apples). When three cooks measure one cup of lettuce, not only will they chop it differently, they will fill the measuring cup differently. The end result will be three different weights for each of the cups. The same goes for apples. A "medium apple" for three cooks will result in three subjective measures, and three different weights.

In this book it was important to include Nutrition Facts in order to give the reader a sense of the nutritional value of each recipe. People with diabetes, for example, are often required to weigh the different foods they eat each day. Providing Nutrition Facts necessitates precision and is an integral part of the overall philosophy of this book of paying close attention to what goes into our bodies.

I have mentioned above the USDA *National Nutrient Database for Standard Reference* (retrieved June 3, 2013 from http://ndb.nal.usda.gov/ndb/search/list). It is the standardized reference for weight, volume and nutrition facts of most ingredients. I used this tool when preparing the recipes. It is very helpful in calculating the approximate quantities that you need for each recipe. These approximate quantities are given in parentheses in each recipe after the exact measurements of weight or volume. However, there were instances in which I did not find useful measurements for the ingredients (e.g., kabocha, butternut, acorn and spaghetti squashes), or the ingredients were not mentioned (e.g., bean sprouts) in the USDA list. In those cases no approximate quantities were given to the recipes, only the accurate ones.

It's important to note here that the USDA tool tends to be on the light side, and if you factor in peeling and cleaning, it's a good idea to prepare a bit more than the amount listed in the recipe. Also keep in mind that the USDA table often lists the same ingredient in different categories: raw, cooked, peeled, or frozen. In this book, the ingredients in the recipes are usually raw and cleaned, unless otherwise indicated. For quantities, I used the same descriptors as the ones in the USDA table; for example, "leaves" for lettuce or "sprigs" for parsley.

All of the measurements are of the ingredients after they are cleaned and ready for cooking. For example, one pound of squash means the net weight of the squash after it has been peeled and cleaned.

The following example is for GREEN SALAD (page 24)

3oz (85g) (1) cucumber (with peel)
2oz (60g) (4 leaves) lettuce
1.4oz (40g) (2/3 cup chopped) parsley
0.70oz (19g) (2/3 cup) spinach leaves
dash (0.01oz, 0.25g) sea salt

The USDA table lists "one cucumber with peel, raw" (8-1/4"), and that is 10.62 ounces (301 grams). The recipe calls for 3 ounces (85g), so the reader would need to prepare in advance one cucumber for the recipe.

SALADS

Opposite Page: Green Salad, p. 24

GREEN SALAD

Ingredients for 1 portion:

3oz (85g) (1/3, with peel, raw, 8 ¼ inches long) cucumber
2oz (60g) (3 green outer leaves) lettuce
1.4oz (40g) (2/3 cup chopped) parsley, chopped
0.70oz (19g) (2/3 cup) spinach leaves
dash (0.01oz, 0.25g) sea salt

Coarsely chop the lettuce and spinach.
Finely chop the cucumber and parsley.
Mix with salt in a mixing bowl.
Optional: add the juice of half a lemon.

Nutrition facts:
Portions: 1ount per portion:

Calories 40	Fat Cal. 5	**Total Fat** 0.5g (1%DV)
Sat. Fat 0g (0%DV)	*Trans* Fat 0g	**Cholest.** 0mg (0%DV)
Sodium 150mg (6%DV)	**Total carb.** 8g (3%DV)	Fiber 3g (12%DV)
Sugars 2g	**Protein** 3g	Vitamin A (190%DV)
Vitamin C (120%DV)	Calcium (10%DV)	Iron (20%DV)

Percent Daily Values (DV) are based on a 2,000 calorie diet

AVOCADO-CUCUMBER SALAD

Ingredients for 2 portions:

8oz (230g) (1 cup, California, pureed) avocado, Hass
6oz (170g) (2/3 with peel, raw, 8 ¼ inches long) cucumber (with peel)
1 large egg, boiled
0.70oz (20g) (2 ¼ cups, sprigs) dill, finely chopped

Peel cucumber and avocado.
Slice cucumber and cut avocado into small cubes.
Slice boiled egg.
Finely chop dill.
Mix in a small mixing bowl and serve.

Variations:
Prepare without dill.

Nutrition facts:
Portions: 2
Amount per Portion:

Calories 240	Fat Cal. 170	**Total Fat** 19g (30%DV)
Sat. Fat 3.5g (16%DV)	*Trans* Fat 0g	**Cholest.** 105mg (35%DV)
Sodium 45mg (2%DV)	**Total carb.** 14g (5%DV)	Fiber 8g (33%DV)
Sugars 2g	**Protein** 6g	Vitamin A (25%DV)
Vitamin C (35%DV)	Calcium (6%DV)	Iron (10%DV)

Percent Daily Values (DV) are based on a 2,000 calorie diet

POPCORN SALAD

Ingredients for 3 portions:

1/3 cup (5.2oz, 150g) popcorn, organic
3.50oz (100g) (1 small, with skin) Granny Smith apple
1oz (28g) (2 green outer leaves) lettuce
4oz (115g) (½ cup, California, pureed) Hass avocado

Please note: There is no oil or salt used in this recipe!
Spread the popcorn in one layer in a heavy-bottomed pot. Cover the pot. Cook on medium heat. Listen to the popcorn as it starts popping. When the popping becomes steady lower the flame to medium-low.
Take the pot off the heat immediately after the popcorn stops popping to prevent burning.
Transfer the popcorn to mixing bowl.
Cut the apple into small cubes.
Chop the lettuce and the avocado.
Add apple, lettuce and avocado to the bowl and mix.

Tip: Add fresh lemon juice to the salad to preserve the color of the apple and avocado and to add a tart flavor.

Nutrition facts:
Portions: 3
Amount per portion:

Calories 270	Fat Cal. 70	**Total Fat** 8g (12%DV)
Sat. Fat 1g (6%DV)	*Trans* Fat 0g	**Cholest.** 0mg (0%DV)
Sodium 10mg (0%DV)	**Total carb.** 45g (15%DV)	Fiber 10g (39%DV)
Sugars 4g	**Protein** 6g	Vitamin A (15%DV)
Vitamin C (10%DV)	Calcium (2%DV)	Iron (10%DV)

Percent Daily Values (DV) are based on a 2,000 calorie diet

YAM & SWEET POTATO GREEN SALAD

Ingredients for 2 portions:

8oz (230g) (1 2/3 cups, cubes, raw) yams, baked, peeled
8oz (230g) (1 2/3 cups, cubes, raw) sweet potato, baked, peeled
2oz (60g) (3 green outer leaves) lettuce
7oz (200g) (2 small, with skin) Granny Smith apples, unpeeled
½ cup (0.28oz, 8g) popcorn, organic, popped (without oil or salt)

Mash the yam and the sweet potato (see Baked Yams and Sweet Potatoes, p. 104).
Cut small the lettuce and the apple and mix together.
Add to the yam and sweet potato.
Add the popcorn (see Popcorn Salad for popcorn preparation without oil or salt, p. 26)

TIP: Suggested topping: Add half an avocado with a boiled egg on top for color and taste.

Nutrition facts:
Portions: 2
Amount per portion:

Calories 300	Fat Cal. 5	**Total Fat** 0.5g (1%DV)
Sat. Fat 0g (0%DV)	*Trans* Fat 0g	**Cholest** 0mg (0%DV)
Sodium 60mg (2%DV)	**Total carb.** 72g (24%DV)	Fiber 11g (46%DV)
Sugars 18g	**Protein** 5g	Vitamin A (480%DV)
Vitamin C (80%DV)	Calcium (8%DV)	Iron (10%DV)

Percent Daily Values (DV) are based on a 2,000 calorie diet

SOUPS

Opposite Page: Chicken Soup, p. 38

CAULIFLOWER SOUP

Ingredients for 12 portions:

1lb 5oz (600g) (47) cauliflower florets
1lb 1oz (480g) (2 ½ medium) zucchini
5oz (145g) (15 medium) baby carrots
6 cups (48fl oz, 1421ml) water
½ tsp (0.11oz, 3g) sea salt
2 large eggs

Coarsely chop the vegetables.
Add the salt to the water and bring to a boil.
Add the vegetables to the boiling water and cook on a low/medium flame.
Beat raw eggs with a fork, bring the water to boil again and add the eggs.
Lower the heat to low/medium and mix the soup to thicken it with the egg.
Cook to desired thickness.

Tip: To smooth the soup, lower the heat and puree the soup with a hand blender.

Nutrition facts:
Portions: 12
Amount per portion:

Calories 40	Fat Cal. 10	**Total Fat** 1g (2%DV)
Sat. Fat 0g (0%DV)	*Trans* Fat 0g	**Cholest.** 35mg (12%DV)
Sodium 135mg (6%DV)	**Total carb.** 5g (2%DV)	Fiber 2g (9%DV)
Sugars 3g	**Protein** 3g	Vitamin A (35%DV)
Vitamin C (90%DV)	Calcium (4%DV)	Iron (4%DV)

Percent Daily Values (DV) are based on a 2,000 calorie diet

CORN SOUP

Ingredients for 8 portions:

5 cups (40fl oz, 1184ml) water
½ tbsp (0.11oz, 3g) sea salt
9oz (255g) (1 1/3 medium) zucchini
6oz (170g) (17 medium) baby carrots
5oz (146g) (11) cauliflower florets
½ lb (227g) frozen corn
3 large eggs
4.5 tbsp (1.95oz, 55g) polenta
0.71oz (20g) (1/3 cup) parsley

Add salt to the water and bring to a boil.
Coarsely chop the zucchini, baby carrots and cauliflower and cook in the boiling water.
Lower the heat and puree with a hand blender until the soup is smooth.
Increase the heat and add the frozen corn.
In a small bowl beat the eggs and then add into the boiling soup.
Add the polenta and cook until soup is thick but not too thick.
Coarsely chop the parsley and add in the final 3 minutes of cooking.

Tip: Top with dried edamame or organic popcorn (see recipe for Popcorn Salad, p. 26, for preparing no-salt, no-oil organic popcorn).

Nutrition facts:
Portions: 8
Amount per portion:

Calories 100	Fat Cal. 20	**Total Fat** 2.5g (4%DV)
Sat. Fat 0.5g (3%DV)	*Trans* Fat 0g	**Cholest.** 80mg (26%DV)
Sodium 200mg (9%DV)	**Total carb.** 15g (5%DV)	Fiber 2g (9%DV)
Sugars 3g	**Protein** 5g	Vitamin A (70%DV)
Vitamin C (45%DV)	Calcium (4%DV)	Iron (8%DV)

Percent Daily Values (DV) are based on a 2,000 calorie diet

SPINACH AND CORN SOUP

Ingredients for 8 portions:

2 2/3 cups (21fl oz, 609ml) water
1tsp (0.21oz, 6g) sea salt
1 lb (454g) (2 ½ cups) chopped frozen spinach
1 lb (454g) (3 cups) frozen corn
3 tbsp (0.89 oz, 25g) fine corn flour
1.41oz (40 g) (4 ½ cups, sprigs) dill
1.41oz (40 g) (2/3 cup) parsley

Add the salt to the water and bring to a boil.
Add the frozen spinach and corn.
Thicken with the fine corn flour.
Coarsely chop the dill and parsley and add in the final three 3 minutes of cooking.

Tip: Top with organic popcorn (see Popcorn Salad, p. 26, for preparation of no-oil, no-salt organic popcorn).

Nutrition facts:
Portions: 8
Amount per portion:

Calories 80	Fat Cal. 10	**Total Fat** 1g (2%DV)
Sat. Fat 0g (0%DV)	*Trans* Fat 0g	**Cholest.** 0mg (0%DV)
Sodium 350mg (15%DV)	**Total carb.** 18g (6%DV)	Fiber 4g (16%DV)
Sugars 0g	**Protein** 5g	Vitamin A (150%DV)
Vitamin C (25%DV)	Calcium (10%DV)	Iron (10%DV)

Percent Daily Values (DV) are based on a 2,000 calorie diet

VEGETABLE SOUP

Ingredients for 8 portions:

---

4 cups (32fl oz, 947ml) water
1 tsp (0.21oz, 6g) salt
10oz (285g) (22) cauliflower florets
10oz (285g) (1½ medium) zucchini
5oz (140g) carrots
1oz (28g) broccoli florets
3 large eggs
1.4oz (40g) (2/3 cup) parsley
0.71oz (20g) (2¼ cup, sprigs) dill

Add salt to the water and bring to a boil.
Coarsely chop the cauliflower, zucchini, carrots and broccoli and add to the water. Cook on medium heat.
In a small bowl, beat the eggs, and then add to the boiling soup while stirring with a wooden spoon.
Lower to medium heat and cook until the vegetables are tender.
Coarsely chop the parsley and dill and add in the last 3 minutes of cooking time.

Tip: Use a hand blender to shred the cooked vegetables for a finer texture before you add the eggs. If desired, add 2 tbsp of fine corn flour for thickening.

Nutrition facts:
Portions: 8
Amount per portion:

Calories 90	Fat Cal. 20	**Total Fat** 2.5g (4%DV)
Sat. Fat 0.5g (3%DV)	*Trans* Fat 0g	**Cholest.** 80mg (26%DV)
Sodium 350mg (14%DV)	**Total carb.** 13g (4%DV)	Fiber 3g (12%DV)
Sugars 3g	**Protein** 6g	Vitamin A (70%DV)
Vitamin C (80%DV)	Calcium (6%DV)	Iron (8%DV)

Percent Daily Values (DV) are based on a 2,000 calorie diet

SQUASH SOUP

Ingredients for 10 portions:

2 lbs 1oz (936g) spaghetti squash
2 lbs 1oz (936g) butternut squash
8oz (227g) acorn squash
8oz (227g) (23 medium) baby carrots
4 cups (32f.l oz, 947ml) water
0.11oz (3g) sea salt
4 large eggs
3oz (85g) (1½ cups) parsley

Preheat the oven to 450F.
Bake the squashes for half an hour and let cool before peeling them and removing the seeds (see Four Types of Squash, p. 101).
Chop the squash into small cubes.
Coarsely chop the carrots.
Add the salt to the water and bring to a boil in a large pot with a lid.
Boil the squash over medium or medium-low heat, covered, until tender.
In a small bowl, beat the eggs. When the soup is boiling, add the eggs, and stir.
Lower the heat to medium-low.
Finely chop the parsley and add to the soup in the last 3 minutes of cooking time.

TIP: Serving suggestion: Add dried edamame, lightly salted, or organic popcorn (see Popcorn Salad, p. 26, for organic popcorn with no added oil or salt).

Nutrition facts:
Portions: 10
Amount per portion:

Calories 110	Fat Cal. 20	**Total Fat** 2.5g (4%DV)
Sat. Fat 0.5g (4%DV)	*Trans* Fat 0g	**Cholest.** 85mg (28%DV)
Sodium 190mg (8%DV)	**Total carb.** 22g (7%DV)	Fiber 3g (13%DV)
Sugars 6g	**Protein** 5g	Vitamin A (290%DV)
Vitamin C (50%DV)	Calcium (10%DV)	Iron (10%DV)

Percent Daily Values (DV) are based on a 2,000 calorie diet

YAM SOUP

Ingredients for 8 portions:

15oz (425g) (3 cups, cubed) yams, baked, peeled and seeded
10oz (292g) (23) cauliflower florets
7oz (200g) broccoli florets
4 cups (32fl oz, 947ml) water
1 tsp (0.21oz, 6g) sea salt
2 large eggs
1.41oz (40g) (2/3 cup) parsley
3tbsp (0.89oz, 25g) fine corn flour

Cut yams into small cubes.
Finely chop cauliflower and broccoli.
Add the salt to the water and bring to a boil.
Add yams first. Cook for 20 minutes on high beat and then lower to medium flame before adding the cauliflower and broccoli.
Add the fine corn flour while stirring with a wooden spoon.
In a small bowl, beat the eggs and then add to the boiling soup while stirring.
Cook for another 10 to 20 minutes, keeping the lid on to preserve the liquids. Stir occasionally.
Check to see if the vegetables are tender.
Finely chop the parsley and add in the last 3 minutes of cooking time.

TIP: Serving suggestion: Top with dry edamame or organic popcorn (see Popcorn Salad, p. 26, for preparation of no-oil, no-salt organic popcorn).
For a smooth texture, use a hand blender after you add the fine corn flour and before you add the eggs.

Nutrition facts:
Portions: 8
Amount per portion:

Calories 110	Fat Cal. 15	**Total Fat** 1.5g (3%DV)
Sat. Fat 0g (0%DV)	*Trans* Fat 0g	**Cholest.** 55mg (18%DV)
Sodium 330mg (14%DV)	**Total carb.** 21g (7%DV)	Fiber 4g (14%DV)
Sugars 1g	**Protein** 4g	Vitamin A (20%DV)
Vitamin C (110%DV)	Calcium (4%DV)	Iron (6%DV)

Percent Daily Values (DV) are based on a 2,000 calorie diet

SQUASH SOUP WITH WILD SARDINES

Ingredients for 24 portions:

2 lbs (910g) spaghetti squash
2 lbs (910g) butternut squash
½ lb (220g) acorn squash
1.3 lbs (590g) (5.5 cups, chopped, ½-inch pieces) cauliflower
3oz (85g) (1½ cups) parsley
11 cups (88fl oz, 2604ml) water
1 tbsp (0.63oz, 18g) sea salt
5 large eggs
8.75oz (250g) wild sardines in water

Fully bake the three squashes and let cool before peeling and removing the seeds (see Four Types of Squash, p. 101).
Cut the squash into large cubes.
Wash the cauliflower and cut into large cubes. Finely chop the parsley.
Add salt to the water and bring to a boil.
Add the vegetables except for the parsley and cook for 5 minutes.
Lower the heat and puree with a hand blender until smooth.
In a small bowl, beat the eggs and add to the boiling soup while stirring with a wooden spoon.
Lower the heat and keep stirring. Drain the wild sardines, finely chop them and add to the soup.
Add the parsley in the last 3 minutes of cooking time.

TIP: Add water sparingly to make the soup thinner, or let it cook longer if it is too thin for your taste. I have found that the best consistency for this soup is when it is not too thick or too thin. It is a good idea to let the soup sit for a few hours before serving to absorb all the flavors.
Serve warm and top with either dried edamame or organic popcorn (see Popcorn Salad, p. 26).

Nutrition facts:
Portions: 24
Amount per portion:

Calories 70	Fat Cal. 15	**Total Fat** 1.5g (3%DV)
Sat. Fat 0.5g (3%DV)	*Trans* Fat 0g	**Cholest.** 55mg (18%DV)
Sodium 360mg (15%DV)	**Total carb.** 10g (3%DV)	Fiber 2g (7%DV)
Sugars 3g	**Protein** 5g	Vitamin A (90%DV)
Vitamin C (60%DV)	Calcium (10%DV)	Iron (6%DV)

Percent Daily Values (DV) are based on a 2,000 calorie diet

CHICKEN SOUP

Ingredients for 18 portions:

---

6 cups (48fl oz, 1421ml) water
½ tsp (0.11oz, 3g) sea salt
2 ¼ lbs (1022g) chicken back & neck
1 lb 11oz (775g) (78 medium) baby carrots
1 lb 11oz (775g) (4 medium) zucchini, finely chopped
2oz (57g) (2/3 cup) parsley, finely chopped

Put salt, water and chicken in a pot, and simmer for 20 minutes.
Pour the stock through a fine sieve.
Remove the chicken from the pot and place it on a cutting board. Remove the meat from the bones.
Add the stock and the chicken back to the pot.
Add baby carrots and bring to a boil. Simmer for 10 minutes, stirring occasionally.
Add the zucchini and parsley and simmer for another 5 minutes, stirring occasionally.

Tip: Top with a sprig of fresh parsley to add color and enhance taste.

Nutrition facts:
Portions: 18
Amount per portion:

Calories 160	Fat Cal. 60	**Total Fat** 7g (11%DV)
Sat. Fat 2g (9%DV)	*Trans* Fat 0g	**Cholest.** 45mg (16%DV)
Sodium 150mg (6%DV)	**Total carb.** 5g (2%DV)	Fiber 2g (7%DV)
Sugars 3g	**Protein** 18g	Vitamin A (130%DV)
Vitamin C (20%DV)	Calcium (4%DV)	Iron (8%DV)

Percent Daily Values (DV) are based on a 2,000 calorie diet

VEGETARIAN DISHES

Opposite Page: Zucchini, Carrots and Brown Rice, p. 45

COOKED YAMS, ZUCCHINI, AND APPLES

Ingredients for 6 portions:

23oz (652g) (4¼ cups, cubed) yams
17oz (482g) (2½ medium) zucchini
7oz (200g) (2 small, with skin) Granny Smith apples
1 tsp (0.22oz, 6g) sea salt
½ cup (4floz, 118ml) water
3 large eggs
1 cup (3.14oz, 89g) dried edamame

Cut yams, zucchini and apple into small cubes.
Add salt to water and bring to a boil in a non-stick casserole.
Add yams, zucchini and apple.
When the ingredients are steaming and there is not much water left, beat the eggs and add to the mix.
Cook until the water evaporates and yams are tender.

Nutrition facts:
Portions: 6
Amount per portion:

Calories 260	Fat Cal. 45	**Total Fat** 5g (8%DV)
Sat. Fat 1g (6%DV)	*Trans* Fat 0g	**Cholest.** 105mg (35%DV)
Sodium 530mg (22%DV)	**Total carb.** 43g (14%DV)	Fiber 10g (40%DV)
Sugars 7g	**Protein** 13g	Vitamin A (10%DV)
Vitamin C (60%DV)	Calcium (6%DV)	Iron (15%DV)

Percent Daily Values (DV) are based on a 2,000 calorie diet

SEARED ZUCCHINI WITH AVOCADO

Ingredients for 4 portions:

---

2 large eggs
2 lbs (910g) (4 2/3 medium) zucchini
8oz (230g) (1 cup, California, pureed) ripe avocado, Hass
½ tsp (0.11oz, 3g) sea salt

Boil the eggs, peel and slice.
Wash and slice the zucchini.

In a non-stick casserole, add salt and sear the zucchini on medium heat, stirring constantly with a wooden spoon, for about three minutes. Do not over-cook. Let cool in a colander to allow the draining of the excess water from the zucchini. Cut the avocado into small cubes.
Add the sliced boiled egg and the avocado to the zucchini and mix.
Tip: Top with a few thin slices of Granny Smith apple to add tartness.

Nutrition facts:
Portions: 4
Amount per portion:

Calories 140	Fat Cal. 80	**Total Fat** 9g (14%DV)
Sat. Fat 2g (10%DV)	*Trans* Fat 0g	**Cholest.** 105mg (35%DV)
Sodium 360mg (15%DV)	**Total carb.** 12g (4%DV)	Fiber 5g (22%DV)
Sugars 7g	**Protein** 7g	Vitamin A (15%DV)
Vitamin C (80%DV)	Calcium (6%DV)	Iron (8%DV)

Percent Daily Values (DV) are based on a 2,000 calorie diet

ZUCCHINI, AVOCADO AND SPINACH

Ingredients for 8 portions:

2 large eggs, boiled
2 lbs 2oz (964g) (5 medium) zucchini
½ tsp (0.11oz, 3g) sea salt
¼ cup (2fl oz, 59ml) water
1 lb (454g) frozen spinach, shredded
8oz (227g) (1 cup, California, pureed) ripe avocado, Hass

Boil the eggs, peel and slice.
Wash and slice the zucchini.
Steam the zucchini for 15-20 minutes, until it becomes tender. Let cool in a mixing bowl.
Add just enough water to cover the bottom of the cooking pot, put in the salt, bring to a boil and add the frozen spinach. Cook until spinach is soft. Simmer until most of the water evaporates.
Do not overcook in order to prevent the spinach from sticking to the bottom of the pot. Let cool.
Cut the avocado into small cubes.
Mix all of the ingredients in a mixing bowl.
Serve warm or cold.

TIP: This is a light dish that goes well with either polenta or baked corn-on-the cob (see recipes, pp. 54 and 102, respectively).

Nutrition facts:
Portions: 8
Amount per portion:

Calories 100	Fat Cal. 50	**Total Fat** 6g (9%DV)
Sat. Fat 1g (5%DV)	*Trans* Fat 0g	**Cholest.** 55mg (18%DV)
Sodium 210mg (9%DV)	**Total carb.** 9g (3%DV)	Fiber 5g (21%DV)
Sugars 3g	**Protein** 6g	Vitamin A (140%DV)
Vitamin C (15%DV)	Calcium (10%DV)	Iron (10%DV)

Percent Daily Values (DV) are based on a 2,000 calorie diet

ZUCCHINI, CARROTS AND BROWN RICE

Ingredients for 4 portions:

---

1 lb (454g) carrots
1 lb (454g) (2¼ medium) zucchini
3 oz (85g) broccoli florets
½ tsp (0.11oz, 3g) sea salt
2 cups (16 floz, 474g) water
2 cups (13.76oz, 390g) brown rice, cooked (see Brown Rice, p. 107)
2 large eggs, boiled

Slice the carrots, zucchini and broccoli florets.
Slice the boiled eggs.
Add the salt to the water and bring to a boil in a covered non-stick casserole, stirring occasionally with a wooden spoon.
Add the carrots and cook for 5 minutes in the boiling soup.
Add the zucchini and broccoli and cook for 3 minutes.
Remove the casserole from the stove and drain the vegetables in a colander. It is a good idea to wear gloves to protect your hands from the hot steam. Put the vegetables back into the casserole on medium-low.
Add the cooked brown rice and the sliced boiled eggs and stir with a wooden spoon until the rice warms up and there is no water left at the bottom.
Serve warm.

TIP: Serve with a green salad.

Nutrition facts:
Portions: 4
Amount per portion:

Calories 240	Fat Cal. 40	**Total Fat** 4.5g (7%DV)
Sat. Fat 1g (6%DV)	*Trans* Fat 0g	**Cholest.** 105mg (35%DV)
Sodium 470mg (20%DV)	**Total carb.** 41g (14%DV)	Fiber 6g (25%DV)
Sugars 9g	**Protein** 11g	Vitamin A (390%DV)
Vitamin C (210%DV)	Calcium (15%DV)	Iron (15%DV).

Percent Daily Values (DV) are based on a 2,000 calorie diet

ZUCCHINI, CARROTS AND TWO KINDS OF RICE

Ingredients for 4 portions:

1 lb (454g) (2¼ medium) zucchini
1 lb (454g) carrots
1.5oz (43g) (½ cup) parsley
21oz (595g) (46) cauliflower florets
2 cups (16floz, 474g) water
½ tsp (0.11oz, 3g) sea salt
2 cups (13.76oz, 390g) long-grain white rice, cooked
1 cup (5.64oz, 160g) wild rice, cooked (see Wild Rice, p. 107)

Preheat the oven to 450F.
Slice the zucchini and carrots and mince the parsley.
Spread the zucchini and cauliflower on parchment paper and bake for 25 minutes on the middle shelf. Do not over bake.
Add the salt to the water and bring to a boil in a nonstick casserole with a lid.
Cook the carrots for 5 minutes in the casserole, covered, stirring occasionally with a wooden spoon.
Remove the casserole from the stove and drain the vegetables in a colander. It is a good idea to wear gloves to protect your hands from the hot steam.
When the zucchini and cauliflower are tender, take them out of the oven and add to the casserole. Add the rice and wild rice to the casserole, cook on a medium-low heat, stirring with a wooden spoon, until warm and there is no water left. Do not overcook. Take the casserole off the stove, let cool for 5 minutes and mix in the parsley.
Serve warm.

TIP: Serve with slices of baked yams and sweet potatoes.

Nutrition facts:
Portions: 4
Amount per portion:

Calories 270	Fat Cal. 15	**Total Fat** 1.5g (2%DV),
Sat. Fat 0g (0%DV)	*Trans* Fat 0g	**Cholest.** 0mg (0%DV),
Sodium 760mg (32%DV)	**Total carb.** 57g (19%DV)	Fiber 9g (35%DV),
Sugars 12g	**Protein** 9g	Vitamin A (340%DV),
Vitamin C (180%DV)	Calcium (15%DV)	Iron (20%DV).

Percent Daily Values (DV) are based on a 2,000 calorie diet

TEXTURED VEGETABLE PROTEIN (TVP) AND ZUCCHINI

Note: TVP is made from de-fatted soy flour. It is highly nutritious and contains dietary fiber, iron, magnesium and phosphorus.

Ingredients for 4 portions:

---

2 large eggs
19oz (540g) (2¾ medium) zucchini
7oz (200g) (2 cups, chopped, ½-inch pieces) cauliflower
5oz (142g) broccoli florets
3oz (85g) (9 medium) baby carrots
½ tsp (0.11oz, 3g) sea salt
½ cup (4fl oz, 118ml) water
8oz (227g) (1 cup, California, pureed) ripe avocado, Hass
1 cup (3.35oz, 95g) TVP, hydrated

Boil the eggs and peel.
Dice the zucchini, cauliflower, broccoli and carrots.
Salt the water and add the chopped vegetables.
Cook with a lid for 10 minutes.
Take the lid off and keep cooking to reduce the amount of liquid.
Turn off the heat and drain any remaining liquid. Let cool for 10 minutes.
Slice the boiled eggs and cut the avocado into cubes.
Add the eggs, avocado and the hydrated TVP to the vegetables and mix.
Serve warm.

TIP: Towards the end of cooking, stir constantly in order to make sure that all liquid is cooked off, so the dish will not be soggy. Do not overcook.

Nutrition facts:
Portions: 4
Amount per portion:

Calories 170	Fat Cal. 60	**Total Fat** 7g (11%DV)
Sat. Fat 1.5g (7%DV)	*Trans* Fat 0g	**Cholest.** 70mg (23%DV)
Sodium 260mg (11%DV)	**Total carb.** 15g (5%DV)	Fiber 7g (29%DV)
Sugars 6g,	**Protein** 13g	Vitamin A (60%DV)
Vitamin C (120%DV)	Calcium (10%DV)	Iron (20%DV)

Percent Daily Values (DV) are based on a 2,000 calorie diet

YAMS AND SWEET POTATOES

Ingredients for 6 portions:

14oz (400g) carrots
1 lb 15oz (880g) (6 cups, cubed) yams
1 lb 14oz (850g) (6 ½ cups, cubed) sweet potatoes
1oz (28g) (3 dried, uncooked, pitted) prunes, organic
3oz (85g) broccoli
3oz (85g) (3 cups) spinach leaves
3oz (85g) dill
3oz (85g) parsley
½ tsp (0.11oz, 3g) sea salt
½ cup (4fl oz, 118ml) water
4 large eggs

Shred the carrots, yams and sweet potatoes in a food processor.
Chop the broccoli florets, discarding the stems.
Mince the spinach, parsley and dill.
Put all of the ingredients, except for the parsley, dill, and eggs, in a non-stick casserole with a lid.
Add salt to the water, bring to a boil and then lower the heat to a simmer.
When the vegetables start steaming, beat the eggs and add to the mixture.
Cook for 45 minutes, stirring occasionally.
Check that the yams and sweet potatoes are tender.
Add the parsley and dill in the last 3 minutes.
Serve warm.

TIP: Top with freshly cut, whole sprigs of parsley.

Nutrition facts:
Portions: 6
Amount per portion:

Calories 400	Fat Cal. 35	**Total Fat** 4g (6%DV)
Sat. Fat 1g (6%DV)	*Trans* Fat 0g	**Cholest.** 140mg (47%DV)
Sodium 420mg (18%DV)	**Total carb.** 83g (28%DV)	Fiber 14g (54%DV)
Sugars 10g	**Protein** 11g	Vitamin A (670%DV)
Vitamin C (130%DV)	Calcium (20%DV)	Iron (30%DV)

Percent Daily Values (DV) are based on a 2,000 calorie diet

SEARED YAMS, SWEET POTATOES AND ZUCCHINI

Ingredients for 8 portions:

15oz (425g) (3 cups, cubed) yams
15oz (425g) (3 ¼ cups, cubed) sweet potatoes
1 lb 9oz (710g) (3 2/3 medium) zucchini
4 large eggs, divided
1 lb 4oz (570g) (5 1/3 cups, chopped, ½-inch pieces) cauliflower
8oz (230g) carrots, diced
½ tsp sea salt (0.11oz, 3g)

Note: The yams and sweet potatoes are seared separately from the rest since they are cooked at a slower pace than the other ingredients.

Cut lengthwise and then across the yams, sweet potatoes and zucchini.
Beat the eggs and pour into a mixing bowl with the yams and sweet potatoes.
Cook the yams and sweet potatoes on medium heat in a non-stick casserole with a lid.
Mix with a wooden spoon until the ingredients begin to brown.
Let cool in a mixing bowl.
Chop the cauliflower and carrots and put in a fresh mixing bowl with the zucchini.
Scramble the remaining two eggs, add salt, and add to the mix.
Pour into the casserole and sear until brown.
Turn off the heat and mix with the already seared yams and sweet potatoes.
Serve warm.

Tip: Top with freshly cut slices of avocado.

Nutrition facts:
Portions: 8
Amount per Portion:

Calories 190	Fat Cal. 30	**Total Fat** 3g (5%DV)
Sat. Fat 1g (5%DV)	*Trans* Fat 0g	**Cholest.** 105mg (35%DV)
Sodium 260mg (11%DV)	**Total carb.** 34g (11%DV)	Fiber 7g (28%DV)
Sugars 8g	**Protein** 7g	Vitamin A (240%DV)
Vitamin C (100%DV)	Calcium (8%DV)	Iron (10%DV)

Percent Daily Values (DV) are based on a 2,000 calorie diet

YAM AND SWEET POTATO PATTIES

Ingredients for 12 patties:

---

1 lb 7oz (650g) (4 1/3 cups, cubed) yams
1 lb 6oz (630g) (4 ¾ cups, cubed) sweet potatoes
3 large eggs
½ tsp (0.11oz, 3 g) sea salt
1 cup (7 oz, 200 g) polenta (or coarse cornmeal)

Shred the yams and sweet potatoes in a food processor.
Beat the eggs with the salt and add to the yams and potatoes.
Make the mixtures into patties, coat with the polenta, and sear on both sides in a non-stick casserole.
Serve warm.

Tip: Instead of eggs you can use 12 oz (340 g) of unsweetened applesauce.

Nutrition facts:
Patties: 12
Amount per Portion:

Calories 190	Fat Cal. 15	**Total Fat** 1.5g (2%DV)
Sat. Fat 0g (0%DV)	*Trans* Fat 0g	**Cholest.** 55mg (18%DV)
Sodium 150mg (6%DV)	**Total carb.** 39g (13%DV)	Fiber 4g (15%DV)
Sugars 3g	**Protein** 5g	Vitamin A (150%DV)
Vitamin C (20%DV)	Calcium (4%DV)	Iron (8%DV)

Percent Daily Values (DV) are based on a 2,000 calorie diet

BROWN RICE EMPANADAS

Ingredients for 8 empanadas:

For the dough:
1 cup (6.53oz, 185g) brown rice flour
1 large egg
1 dash sea salt
½ cup (4fl oz, 118ml) water

For baking:
½ cup (2.79oz, 79g) coarse cornmeal
1 large egg white (for sealing the empanadas)

For the filling:
¾ cup (5.16oz, 146g) brown rice, long-grain, cooked
¼ cup (1.41oz, 40g) seedless raisins

Put baking stones on the bottom shelf and heat the oven to 500F. Take out the middle shelf for better access to the lower shelf.
Alternatively, if you do not have baking stones, put a flat, heavy, all metal skillet on the bottom shelf and heat the oven to 500F.
In both cases, use baking mitts to protect your hands.

To prepare the dough:
Put all of the ingredients for the dough in the bowl of a mixer, and beat with the paddle on low speed until the dough begins to cling to the paddle.
Remove dough from the mixer bowl.

Knead into a ball and then shape into a round about 1 inch thick.
Divide the dough into eight pieces and form into balls.
Put in a bowl and cover with a damp kitchen towel.

Spread coarse corn meal liberally on a clean smooth surface.
Place four of the dough balls on the surface, leaving enough space to roll them out. Each empanada will be about 5 inches in diameter.
Gently roll out each piece of dough, rolling in only one direction, not back and forth, so as not to overstretch the dough.

Using a pastry scraper, work on one empanada at a time:
Gently lift the edge of each empanada with the sharp edge of the pastry scraper, releasing the dough from the surface, and then using the scraper to lift the dough.

If you have not separated the egg white from the yolk in the second egg, now is the time.
Brush the edges of the empanada with the egg white.

Spoon the filling onto the empanada just off-center, so that one side of the filling is touching the center line. Fill the remaining three empanadas.

Using the scraper, fold the empanadas and seal the edges.

Brush the egg white onto the top of the empanadas.

Dust a wooden pizza peel or wide metal spatula with coarse cornmeal. Place the empanadas on the peel (the peel should be big enough to hold three or four empanadas).

Using baking gloves to hold the peel or the spatula, slide the prepared empanadas onto the baking stones.

Bake for 6 to 7 minutes (depending on the filling) and then turn the empanadas with a spatula and bake them on the other side for another 6 to 7 minutes. Be careful not to burn the dough.

Repeat the above with the rest of the dough.

Serve warm or cold.

TIP. Try these fillings:
½ cup brown rice with shredded carrots
½ cup brown rice with yellowfin tuna
½ cup diced zucchini with minced parsley

Nutrition facts:
Portion: 1 empanada
Amount per empanada

Calories 160	Fat Cal. 15	**Total Fat** 1.5g (3%DV)
Sat. Fat 0g (0%DV)	*Trans* Fat 0g	**Cholest.** 25mg (9%DV)
Sodium 40mg (2%DV)	**Total carb.** 33g (11%DV)	Fiber 2g (7%DV)
Sugars 4g	**Protein** 4g	Vitamin A (0%DV)
Vitamin C (0%DV)	Calcium (2%DV)	Iron (6%DV)

Percent Daily Values (DV) are based on a 2,000 calorie diet

POLENTA

Ingredients for 4 portions:

---

6 cups (48fl oz, 1421ml) water
½ tsp (0.11oz, 3g) sea salt
2 cups (13.97oz, 396g) polenta

Using a non-stick casserole, salt the water and bring it to a boil.
Add polenta and stir on high heat until it spreads evenly on the bottom of the casserole..
Turn the heat down to low and simmer for 25 minutes. Stir occasionally with a wooden spoon to prevent the mixture from sticking to the sides of the casserole.
After 25 minutes take the pot off the heat and transfer the polenta to a rectangular container.
Let cool.
Cut into squares and serve warm.

Serving suggestions:
Sear the squares of polenta on both sides in a flat skillet.
Serve with slices of avocado, with or without lemon.
Serve with sunny-side-up egg.
Serve with seared zucchini, lettuce, and avocado.

TIPS:
Polenta is a very forgiving dish. If you cook it 30 minutes instead of 25, it is still excellent. If you stir it only once or twice, it will still come out okay, although it might take on a metallic flavor from the pot. Polenta is usually prepared with butter, margarine, or cheese, but I have chosen to make it fat-free. The nice thing about polenta is that it serves as a binding agent for ingredients such as vegetables. Once the polenta cools it will firm up.

If you do not have a non-stick casserole, add one-fourth cup more water and stir more often. If the polenta sticks to the bottom of the pot, just fill the pot with soapy water and let it soak. The polenta will come out easily after an hour.

You can use different kinds of cornmeal. For example, one-half cup of fine corn flour will yield one and one-half cups of cooked polenta. Cooking time will vary with the mix.

If you do not have any polenta on hand, you can use cornmeal, either medium or coarse, as a substitute. Cooking time will vary.

During cooking you can add 2 tablespoons of defrosted chopped spinach or 2 tablespoons of minced parsley or dill to add flavor.

Nutrition facts:
Portions: 4
Amount per portion:

Calories 370	Fat Cal. 10	**Total Fat** 1.5g (2%DV)
Sat. Fat 0g (0%DV)	*Trans* Fat 0g	**Cholest.** 0mg (0%DV)
Sodium 300mg (12%DV)	**Total carb.** 76g (25%DV)	Fiber 0g (0%DV)
Sugars 0g	**Protein** 8g	Vitamin A (0%DV)
Vitamin C (0%DV)	Calcium (4%DV)	Iron (25%DV)

Percent Daily Values (DV) are based on a 2,000 calorie diet

LIGHT TORTILLAS

Ingredients for 8 tortillas:

---

2 ½ cups (11.82oz, 335g) fine corn flour
5 ¾ cups (46fl oz, 1362ml) water
½ tsp (0.11oz, 3g) sea salt

You will find a recipe for regular tortillas in this book, as well. The recipe here is for much lighter tortillas. I like to use these for wraps.

Prepare two mixing bowls, one for mixing the ingredients, and one for the prepared tortillas. Use a clean damp kitchen towel to line the bowl that will hold the prepared tortillas.

Heat a large non-stick casserole, one with a lid.
Mix all the ingredients in a bowl. The dough will be soupy.
Use a medium-sized scoop to place a portion of the dough onto the bottom of the pan and cover.
When the edges start lifting up and you see long brown streaks, the tortilla is ready to flip. Use a wide flat wooden spatula for this purpose.
Lift the tortilla carefully and flip it to cook on the other side.
Let it cook until you see brown streaks. Do not overcook.
Lift the tortilla with the spatula and place in the bowl with the damp towel. Cover with the towel to keep it fresh.
Serve warm or cold depending on the filling of the wrap.

Nutrition facts:
Tortillas: 8
Amount per tortilla:

Calories 150	Fat Cal. 15	**Total Fat** 1.5g (2%DV)
Sat. Fat 0g (0%DV)	*Trans* Fat 0g	**Cholest.** 0mg (0%DV)
Sodium 150mg (6%DV)	**Total carb.** 32g (11%DV)	Fiber 3g (11%DV)
Sugars 1g	**Protein** 4g	Vitamin A (0%DV),
Vitamin C (0%DV)	Calcium (8%DV)	Iron (4%DV)

Percent Daily Values (DV) are based on a 2,000 calorie diet.

TORTILLAS

Ingredients for 32 tortillas:

For the dough:
4 cups fine corn flour (19.4oz, 550g)
4 cups water
1 large egg
½ tsp (0.11oz, 3g) sea salt

For the coating:
1 cup (6.98oz, 198g) polenta or coarse cornmeal

I prefer to prepare tortillas by hand instead of using a press. I also prefer this version with the egg. It makes the tortillas moister, more "meaty" and less dry to eat. These tortillas are more full-bodied than the Light Tortillas above; they have less liquid content, and once you become proficient in making them, are faster to prepare.

Before you start preparing the dough, please do the following:
Prepare two mixing bowls, one for mixing the ingredients, and one for the prepared tortillas. Use a clean damp kitchen towel to line the bowl that will hold the prepared tortillas and keep them moist.

Put all of the ingredients, except for the coarse cornmeal or polenta, in the bowl of a mixer. Using the paddle, mix on low speed until large lumps of dough are formed.
Continue mixing for another minute.
Take the dough out of the mixer and form a large ball.

Divide the ball into four pieces and then form four balls.
Form four 1-inch rounds.
Using a pastry scraper, score each round into 8 pieces and then slice.
Form each slice into a ball, place in a bowl, and cover with a damp towel.

Heat two large flat skillets on medium flame. You can use only one skillet, but it will easier and faster to work with two.

Prepare a clean work space of about 12 by 12 inches on your counter.
Dust the work space with the coarse cornmeal or polenta.
Remove four dough balls at a time, and flatten them with your hands into rounds about 5 inches in diameter and 2 millimeters or 1/16-inch thick.

Do not overstretch. If the dough tears, it is probably due to trying to stretch it too far.

A tip: If you prefer larger tortillas, simply cut fewer slices of the dough. For example, to double the size of each tortilla, cut the dough into 16 pieces instead of 32.

Dust the top of each tortilla with coarse cornmeal.

Use the sharp edge of a pastry scraper to lift the edges of the tortilla all around until you can easily lift it off the counter. This action is similar to the move you make when you use a spatula to gently lift a sunny-side-up egg from a frying pan.

Dust the skillet with coarse cornmeal. Lift the tortilla from the counter and slide it quickly onto the hot skillet. Lift the remaining three tortillas in the same fashion and slide them, one by one, into the skillet.

Cook for about 30 seconds. Using a wide spatula, flip the tortilla. It should come up easily and should look tan, with speckled dark spots where it was browned by the skillet. Do not overcook. If you sense overcooking, lower the heat or cook for less time. If you are using two skillets, flip the tortilla into the second skillet to cook on the remaining side.

Cook for another 30 seconds, lift with the wide spatula and put into the bowl lined with the towel. Cover the bowl with the edges of a towel so that the tortillas do not dry out. Prepare the rest of the tortillas in the same fashion, working on four balls of dough each time.

TIP: When you become proficient, you will be able to take the next four balls of dough and flatten them on the counter while the first batch is cooking. You will need to work fast so the tortillas are not overcooked.

You can warm up the tortillas in a microwave, but note that this will cook them a bit more, so make sure to keep them moist during the initial cooking. The tortillas can last for few days in the refrigerator if you cover them with a damp towel.
Note: You can also use baking stones to cook the tortillas.
Place the baking stones on the bottom shelf of a cold oven. Heat to 500F (if you have a convection setting, use that).
Dust a pizza peel with polenta.
After you lift the tortillas from the counter with the pastry scraper, place them on the pizza peel and slide them into the oven.
Cook for about 30 seconds. Use the peel to flip the tortillas and bake for another 30 seconds. Follow the same instructions as for baking in a skillet.

Nutrition facts:
Portions: 32
Amount per portion:

Calories 90	Fat Cal. 10	**Total Fat** 1g (1%DV)
Sat. Fat 0g (0%DV)	*Trans* Fat 0g	**Cholest.** 5mg (2%DV)
Sodium 640mg (27%DV)	**Total carb.** 19g (6%DV)	Fiber 1g (5%DV)
Sugars 0g	**Protein** 2g	Vitamin A (0%DV)
Vitamin C (0%DV)	Calcium (2%DV)	Iron (4%DV)

Percent Daily Values (DV) are based on a 2,000 calorie diet

QUICHES

Opposite page: Zucchini and Carrot Quiche, p. 62

ZUCCHINI & CARROT QUICHE

Ingredients for 12 portions:

2 lbs 2oz (950g) (5 medium) zucchini
1 lb 6oz (610g) carrots
2oz (57g) parsley
8 large eggs
1 tsp (0.21oz, 6g) sea salt
1 cup (4.59oz, 130g) wild rice, cooked
7oz (198g) polenta or medium ground cornmeal

Shred vegetables in a food processor
Put in a mixing bowl.
Add eggs, salt, cooked wild rice (see recipe, p. 107) and polenta.
Mix well in the bowl.

Line the sides of a large rectangular baking pan (12 x 17) with strips of baking paper; dampen the paper first so that it will adhere to the sides of the pan. Make sure to leave ½-inch margins on the bottom of the pan.
Line the pan with a silicone baking sheet to prevent the quiche from sticking.

Sprinkle the silicone baking sheet with water.
Spread the polenta evenly on the baking sheet.
Give the ingredients one last mix to make sure the eggs are well distributed and evenly spread the mix in the pan.
Use a pastry scraper to even out the mixture.

Bake at 425F for 28 minutes. Adjust the oven to Broil and broil for one minute.
Open the oven, rotate the pan and broil for another minute. Let cool for 5 minutes.

Put a cutting board on top of the quiche and flip the baking pan onto another cutting board.
Peel off the baking paper first. Starting at a corner and going diagonally, peel off the silicone baking sheet.
The quiche is now upside down. Cover it with the free board and flip it back onto the other board.

Cut and serve warm.

TIP: For topping, add strips of freshly cut avocado.

Nutrition facts:
Portions: 12
Amount per portion:

Calories 150   Fat Cal. 35   **Total Fat** 4g (6%DV)
Sat. Fat 1g (6%DV)   *Trans* Fat 0g   **Cholest.** 140mg (47%DV)
Sodium 290mg (12%DV)   **Total carb.** 22g (7%DV)   Fiber 3g (11%DV)
Sugars 5g   **Protein** 7g   Vitamin A (160%DV)
Vitamin C (35%DV)   Calcium (6%DV)   Iron (15%DV)

Percent Daily Values (DV) are based on a 2,000 calorie diet

ZUCCHINI & YAM QUICHE

Ingredients for 12 portions:

---

1 lb 15oz (880g) (6 cups, cubed) yams
5 lbs 4oz (2kg 380g) (12 medium) zucchini
14oz (400g) (3 small, with skin) Granny Smith apples
12oz (340g) baby carrots
1 tsp (0.21oz, 6g) sea salt
10 large eggs
1½ cups (3.5oz, 100g) polenta or medium ground cornmeal, divided

---

Peel the yams.
Dice the zucchini, yams, apples and carrots, or shred in a food processor using the disk.
Put in a large mixing bowl.
Add salt to the eggs and beat lightly before adding to the mix.
Add ½ cup of polenta to the mix.

Line the sides of a large rectangular baking pan (12 x 17) with strips of baking paper; dampen the paper first so that it will adhere to the sides of the pan. Make sure to leave ½-inch margins on the bottom of the pan.
Line the pan with a silicone baking sheet to prevent the quiche from sticking.

Spread the remaining one cup of polenta evenly on the silicone baking sheet.
Mix the ingredients once more to make sure the eggs are evenly distributed and then spread in the pan. Use a pastry scraper to even out the mixture.

Bake at 450F for 50 minutes: 30 minutes on the bottom shelf and 20 minutes on the middle shelf. The quiche is ready when the yams look golden. Be careful not to overcook. Let cool for 5 minutes.
Put a cutting board on top of the quiche and flip the baking pan onto another cutting board.
Peel off the baking paper first. Starting at a corner and going diagonally, peel off the silicone baking sheet.
The quiche is now upside down. Cover it with the free board and flip it back onto the other board.
Cut and serve warm.

TIP: For topping, add freshly cut avocado with a few drops of lemon.

Nutrition facts:
Portions: 12
Amount per portion:

Calories 300	Fat Cal. 45	**Total Fat** 5g (8%DV)
Sat. Fat 1.5g (8%DV)	*Trans* Fat 0g	**Cholest** 175mg (59%DV)
Sodium 300mg (12%DV)	**Total carb.** 53g (18%DV)	Fiber 7g (26%DV)
Sugars 10g	**Protein** 11g	Vitamin A (90%DV)
Vitamin C (80%DV)	Calcium (8%DV)	Iron (20%DV)

Percent Daily Values (DV) are based on a 2,000 calorie diet

BUTTERNUT QUICHE

Ingredients for 12 portions:

2 lbs 2oz (965g) (5 medium) zucchini
2 lbs (907g) butternut squash, par-baked (see Four Types of Squash, p. 101)
1 lb 5oz (595g) (5.5 cups, chopped, ½-inch pieces) cauliflower florets
4oz (113g) broccoli florets
3oz (85g) parsley
1 tsp (0.21oz, 6g) sea salt
8 large eggs
1 cup (7oz, 198g) polenta or medium ground cornmeal

Slice vegetables in a food processor.
Add the salt to the eggs and mix all ingredients in a mixing bowl, except for the polenta.

Line the sides of a large rectangular baking pan (12 x 17) with strips of baking paper; dampen the paper first so that it will adhere to the sides of the pan. Make sure to leave ½-inch margins on the bottom of the pan.
Line the pan with a silicone baking sheet to prevent the quiche from sticking.
Sprinkle the baking sheet with water.
Spread the polenta evenly on the baking sheet.
Mix the ingredients once more to make sure the eggs are evenly distributed and then spread in the pan. Use a pastry scraper to even out the mixture.

Bake at 425F for 50 minutes: 25 minutes on the bottom shelf and 25 minutes on the middle shelf. Let cool for 5 minutes.

Put a cutting board on top of the quiche and flip the baking pan onto another cutting board.

Peel off the baking paper first. Starting at a corner and going diagonally, peel off the silicone baking sheet.

The quiche is now upside down. Cover it with the free board and flip it back onto the other board.

Cut and serve warm.

TIP: If you do not have butternut squash you can substitute acorn; the baking time might be a bit shorter because the acorn is drier.

Nutrition facts:
Portions: 12
Amount per Portion:

Calories 170	Fat Cal. 35	**Total Fat** 4g (6%DV)
Sat. Fat 1g (6%DV)	*Trans* Fat 0g	**Cholest.** 140mg (47%DV)
Sodium 270mg (11%DV)	**Total carb.** 27g (9%DV)	Fiber 2g (8%DV)
Sugars 5g	**Protein** 9g	Vitamin A (190%DV)
Vitamin C (110%DV)	Calcium (8%DV)	Iron (15%DV)

Percent Daily Values (DV) are based on a 2,000 calorie diet

CAULIFLOWER QUICHE

Ingredients for 12 portions

---

2 lbs 14oz (1300g) (6 ½ medium) zucchini
2 lbs 4oz (1020g) (79) cauliflower florets
1 tsp (0.22oz, 6g) sea salt
8 large eggs
1 cup (7oz, 198g) polenta or medium ground cornmeal

Dice the vegetables and put in a mixing bowl.
Add salt to the eggs and thoroughly mix all ingredients except for the polenta.

Line the sides of a large rectangular baking pan (12 x 17) with strips of baking paper; dampen the paper first so that it will adhere to the sides of the pan. Make sure to leave ½-inch margins on the bottom of the pan.
Line the pan with a silicone baking sheet to prevent the quiche from sticking.

Spread the polenta evenly on the silicone baking sheet.
Mix the ingredients once more to make sure the eggs are evenly distributed and then spread in the pan. Use a pastry scraper to even out the mixture.

Bake at 425F for 25 minutes on the lower shelf and then 25 minutes on the middle one.
Let cool for 5 minutes.

Put a cutting board on top of the quiche and flip the baking pan onto another cutting board.
Peel off the baking paper first. Starting at a corner and going diagonally, peel off the silicone baking sheet.
The quiche is now upside down. Cover it with the free board and flip it back onto the other board.
Cut and serve warm.

TIP: To refrigerate leftovers, put pieces of baking paper between the slices to keep them firm and to make serving easier.

Nutrition facts:
Amount per Portion:
Portions: 12

Calories 150	Fat Cal. 35	**Total Fat** 4g (6%DV)
Sat. Fat 1g (6%DV)	*Trans* Fat 0g	**Cholest.** 140mg (47%DV)
Sodium 270mg (11%DV)	**Total carb.** 22g (7%DV)	Fiber 4g (15%DV)
Sugars 6g	**Protein** 9g	Vitamin A (10%DV)
Vitamin C (160%DV)	Calcium (6%DV)	Iron (15%DV)

Percent Daily Values (DV) are based on a 2,000 calorie diet

YAM AND SWEET POTATO QUICHE

Ingredients for 12 portions

---

1 lb 5oz (600g) (4 ½ cups, cubed) yams, baked & peeled
1 lb 5oz (600g) (5 cups, cubed) sweet potatoes, baked & peeled
4oz (115g) (12 medium) baby carrots
8 large eggs
1 tsp (0.21oz, 6g) sea salt
1 cup (7oz, 198g) polenta or medium ground cornmeal

Mash the peeled yams and sweet potatoes.
Cut zucchini crosswise into thin slices.
Finely dice the carrots.
Add the salt to the eggs and mix all ingredients except for the polenta in a mixing bowl.

Line the sides of a large rectangular baking pan (12 x 17) with strips of baking paper; dampen the paper first so that it will adhere to the sides of the pan. Make sure to leave ½-inch margins on the bottom of the pan.
Line the pan with a silicone baking sheet to prevent the quiche from sticking.

Spread the polenta evenly on the baking sheet.
Mix the ingredients once more to make sure the eggs are evenly distributed and then spread in the pan. Use a pastry scraper to even out the mixture.
Bake at 450F for 10 minutes on the bottom shelf and 15 minutes on the middle shelf. Let cool for 5 minutes.
Put a cutting board on top of the quiche and flip the baking pan onto another cutting board.
Peel off the baking paper first. Starting at a corner and going diagonally, peel off the silicone baking sheet.
The quiche is now upside down. Cover it with the free board and flip it back onto the other board.

Cut and serve warm.

TIP: If the quiche isn't firm enough, lower the temperature to 300F and bake on the middle shelf for another 10 minutes.

Nutrition facts:
Portions: 12
Amount per portion:

Calories 180	Fat Cal. 30	**Total Fat** 3.5g (5%DV)
Sat. Fat 1g (5%DV)	*Trans* Fat 0g	**Cholest.** 125mg (41%DV)
Sodium 250mg (11%DV)	**Total carb.** 31g (10%DV)	Fiber 3g (13%DV)
Sugars 4g	**Protein** 7g	Vitamin A (40%DV)
Vitamin C (10%DV)	Calcium (4%DV)	Iron (10%DV)

Percent Daily Values (DV) are based on a 2,000 calorie diet

KABOCHA & WILD SARDINES QUICHE

Ingredients for 12 portions:

2 lbs 11oz (1210g) (6 medium) zucchini
1 lbs 5oz (600g) Kabocha squash
3oz (85g) (9 medium) baby carrots
2oz (57g) (2/3 cup) parsley
1oz (28g) (1 cup) spinach leaves
8.75oz (250g) wild sardines in water
½ tsp sea salt (0.11oz, 3g)
8 large eggs
1 cup (7oz, 200g) polenta or medium ground cornmeal

Finely chop the vegetables and sardines.
Add salt to the eggs and thoroughly mix all ingredients except for the polenta.

Line the sides of a large rectangular baking pan (12 x 17) with strips of baking paper; dampen the paper first so that it will adhere to the sides of the pan. Make sure to leave ½-inch margins on the bottom of the pan.
Line the pan with a silicone baking sheet to prevent the quiche from sticking.

Spread the polenta evenly on the baking sheet.
Mix the ingredients once more to make sure the eggs are evenly distributed and then spread in the pan. Use a pastry scraper to even out the mixture.

Bake for 20 minutes at 450F on the lower shelf and then 20 minutes on the middle shelf. Let cool for 5 minutes.

Put a cutting board on top of the quiche and flip the baking pan onto another cutting board.
Peel off the baking paper first. Starting at a corner and going diagonally, peel off the silicone baking sheet.
The quiche is now upside down. Cover it with the free board and flip it back onto the other board.
Cut and serve warm.

TIP: Zucchini has a high water content. If the quiche isn't firm enough, bake for additional 5 minutes on the lower shelf and then 5 minutes on the middle shelf (for a total cooking time of 50 minutes).

Nutrition facts:
Portions: 12
Amount per Portion:

Calories 180	Fat Cal. 40	**Total Fat** 4.5g (7%DV)
Sat. Fat 1.5g (7%DV)	*Trans* Fat 0g	**Cholest.** 155mg (52%DV)
Sodium 240mg (10%DV)	**Total carb.** 22g (7%DV)	Fiber 2g (9%DV)
Sugars 3g	**Protein** 12g	Vitamin A (40%DV)
Vitamin C (50%DV)	Calcium (15%DV)	Iron (15%DV)

Percent Daily Values (DV) are based on a 2,000 calorie diet

YELLOWFIN TUNA QUICHE

Ingredients for 12 portions:

---

1 lb (454g) wild yellowfin tuna
21oz (595g) (5.5 cups, chopped, ½-inch pieces) cauliflower
2.5oz (71g) broccoli
17oz (482g) (2½ medium) zucchini
4oz (113g) (12 medium) baby carrots
½ tsp (0.11oz, 3g) sea salt
8 large eggs
1 cup (7oz, 200g) polenta or medium ground cornmeal

Wash the tuna, slice, and cut into small cubes.
Dice the vegetables.
Add the salt to the eggs and mix all ingredients in a mixing bowl, except for the polenta.

Line the sides of a large rectangular baking pan (12 x 17) with strips of baking paper; dampen the paper first so that it will adhere to the sides of the pan. Make sure to leave ½-inch margins on the bottom of the pan.
Line the pan with a silicone baking sheet to prevent the quiche from sticking.

Spread the polenta evenly on the baking sheet.
Mix the ingredients once more to make sure the eggs are evenly distributed and then spread in the pan. Use a pastry scraper to even out the mixture.
Bake at 450F for 18 minutes on the lower shelf and 12 minutes on the middle shelf.
Let cool for 10 minutes.

Put a cutting board on top of the quiche and flip the baking pan onto another cutting board.

Peel off the baking paper first. Starting at a corner and going diagonally, peel off the silicone baking sheet.

The quiche is now upside down. Cover it with the free board and flip it back onto the other board.

Cut and serve warm.

TIP: If you prefer a firmer quiche, bake 20 minutes on the lower shelf and 20 minutes on the middle one. This version is drier and crisper, and it keeps well in the refrigerator. To refrigerate leftovers, put pieces of baking paper between the slices to keep them firm and to make serving easier.

Nutrition facts:
Portions: 12
Amount per portion:

Calories 170	Fat Cal. 35	**Total Fat** 4g (6%DV)
Sat. Fat 1g (6%DV)	*Trans* Fat 0g	**Cholest.** 160mg (53%DV)
Sodium 180mg (8%DV)	**Total carb.** 18g (6%DV)	Fiber 2g (7%DV)
Sugars 3g	**Protein** 16g	Vitamin A (35%DV)
Vitamin C (60%DV)	Calcium (4%DV)	Iron (10%DV)

Percent Daily Values (DV) are based on a 2,000 calorie diet

SPINACH AND CORN QUICHE

Ingredients for 12 portions:

---

1 lb (454g) chopped frozen spinach
1 lb (454g) frozen corn
1 lb 5oz (595g) (5.5 cups, chopped, ½-inch pieces) cauliflower
9oz (255g) broccoli
1 lb 1oz (482g) (2½ medium) zucchini
½ tsp (0.11oz, 3g) sea salt
8 large eggs
1 cup (7oz, 200g) polenta or coarse ground cornmeal

Defrost the spinach and the corn.
Finely chop the vegetables.
Add the salt to the eggs and mix all ingredients in a mixing bowl, except for the polenta.

Line the sides of a large rectangular baking pan (12 x 17) with strips of baking paper; dampen the paper first so that it will adhere to the sides of the pan. Make sure to leave ½-inch margins on the bottom of the pan.
Line the pan with a silicone baking sheet to prevent the quiche from sticking.

Spread the polenta evenly on the silicone baking sheet.
Mix the ingredients once more to make sure the eggs are evenly distributed and then spread in the pan. Use a pastry scraper to even out the mixture.
Bake at 450F for 20 minutes on the lower shelf and 15 minutes on the middle shelf.
Let cool for 10 minutes.

Put a cutting board on top of the quiche and flip the baking pan onto another cutting board.
Peel off the baking paper first. Starting at a corner and going diagonally, peel off the silicone baking sheet.
The quiche is now upside down. Cover it with the free board and flip it back onto the other board.
Cut and serve warm.

TIP: Suggested toppings: fresh avocado, dried edamame, or wild sardines in water.
To refrigerate leftovers, put pieces of baking paper between the slices to keep them firm and to make serving easier.

Nutrition facts:
Portions: 12
Amount per portion:

Calories 180	Fat Cal. 40	**Total Fat** 4.5g (7%DV)
Sat. Fat 1g (6%DV)	*Trans* Fat 0g	**Cholest.** 140mg (47%DV)
Sodium 200mg (8%DV)	**Total carb.** 28g (9%DV)	Fiber 4g (17%DV)
Sugars 4g	**Protein** 11g	Vitamin A (110%DV)
Vitamin C (120%DV)	Calcium (10%DV)	Iron (15%DV)

Percent Daily Values (DV) are based on a 2,000 calorie diet

FISH, CHICKEN AND BEEF

Opposite page: Seared Tuna, p. 84

WILD SARDINES

Ingredients for 2 portions:

4.4oz (125g) wild sardines in water
2 large eggs

Finely chop the sardines.
Mix the sardines with the eggs in a mixing bowl.
Heat up a non-stick skillet on medium.
Cook the sardines on one side, covered, and then flip them to cook the other side.
Serve immediately.

Tip: Top with freshly cut strips of avocado and minced parsley.

Nutrition facts:
Portions: 2
Amount per portion:

Calories 240	Fat Cal. 100	**Total Fat** 11g (17%DV)
Sat. Fat 4g (21%DV)	*Trans* Fat 0g	**Cholest.** 415mg (138%DV)
Sodium 450mg (19%DV)	**Total carb.** 1g (0%DV)	Fiber 0g (0%DV)
Sugars 1g	**Protein** 33g	Vitamin A (8%DV)
Vitamin C (0%DV)	Calcium (60%DV)	Iron (20%DV)

Percent Daily Values (DV) are based on a 2,000 calorie diet

TUNA AND ZUCCHINI OMELET

Ingredients for 4 portions:

10oz (284g) yellowfin tuna
2 lbs 2oz (964g) (5 medium) zucchini
1 tsp (0.21oz, 6g) sea salt
4 large eggs

Heat the oven to 450F.
Rinse the tuna and pat dry with paper towels.
Wrap the tuna in foil, creating a packet.
Bake the tuna at 450F for 25 minutes.
Take out of the oven and let cool by opening the packet.
Chop the tuna.

Finely chop the zucchini.
Add salt to the eggs and mix all ingredients, including the chopped baked tuna in a mixing bowl.
Cook in a non-stick skillet on medium heat. Cook just enough to make sure the eggs are firm and then flip and cook on the other side.
Serve warm.

Tip: Top with strips of freshly cut avocado.

Nutrition facts:
Portions: 4
Amount per portion

Calories 160	Fat Cal. 15	**Total Fat** 1.5g (3%DV)
Sat. Fat 0g (0%DV)	*Trans* Fat 0g	**Cholest.** 40mg (14%DV)
Sodium 160mg (6%DV)	**Total carb.** 8g (3%DV)	Fiber 2g (10%DV)
Sugars 6g	**Protein** 30g	Vitamin A (10%DV)
Vitamin C (70%DV)	Calcium (6%DV)	Iron (8%DV)

Percent Daily Values (DV) are based on a 2,000 calorie diet

SEARED BROCCOLI AND CARROTS WITH WILD SARDINES

Ingredients for 2 portions:

5oz (140g) broccoli florets
8oz (230g) (23 medium) baby carrots
2 large eggs
8.75oz (250g) wild sardines in water

Finely chop the vegetables.
Mix with eggs in a mixing bowl.
Sear in a non-stick casserole on medium heat.
Drain the sardines and dice.
Take the vegetables off the heat and mix in the sardines.
Serve warm.

Tip: It isn't necessary to add salt here because the sardines are naturally salty.

Nutrition facts:
Portions: 2
Amount per portion:

Calories 250	Fat Cal. 45	**Total Fat** 5g (8%DV)
Sat. Fat 2.5g (11%DV)	*Trans* Fat 0g	**Cholest.** 105mg (35%DV)
Sodium 620mg (26%DV)	**Total carb.** 13g (4%DV)	Fiber 3g (13%DV)
Sugars 6g	**Protein** 37g	Vitamin A (360%DV)
Vitamin C (110%DV)	Calcium (70%DV)	Iron (25%DV)

Percent Daily Values (DV) are based on a 2,000 calorie diet

FISH STOCK

1.5 lbs (680g) bones from low-fat fish (halibut or cod)
2 cups water (16fl oz, 474g)
½ tsp (0.11oz, 3g) sea salt
1.4oz (40g) (½ cup) parsley
3.5oz (100g) (10 medium) baby carrots
1.4oz (40g) (4½ cups, sprigs) dill

Put all ingredients in a pot, bring to a boil, and simmer for 25 minutes.
Filter the stock through a fine sieve or colander lined with cheesecloth.
If you do not plan to use the stock right away, let cool and refrigerate in a tightly closed container.

Note: The nutrition facts for this particular fish stock are not listed in the USDA tables or the Nutra Coster software. So I used what I considered to be the closest approximation, which the USDA table calls "06174, soup, stock, fish, home-prepared" (http://ndb.nal.usda.gov/ndb/foods/show/1265).

Nutrition facts for 1 cup (8.47 oz, 240 g) of stock:
Amount per portion

Calories 40	Fat Cal. 15	**Total Fat** 2g (3%DV)
Sat. Fat 0g (0%DV)	*Trans* Fat 0g	**Cholest.** 0mg (0%DV)
Sodium 360mg (15%DV)	**Total carb.** 0g (0%DV)	Fiber 0g (0%DV)
Sugars 0g,	**Protein** 5g	Vitamin A (0%DV)
Vitamin C (0%DV)	Calcium (0%DV)	Iron (0%DV)

Percent Daily Values (DV) are based on a 2,000 calorie diet

BAKED TILAPIA FILET

Ingredients for 2 portions:

---

1 lb (454g) Tilapia filet
20oz (550g) (4 small, with skin) Granny Smith apples
4oz (113g) (12 medium) baby carrots

Heat the oven to 450F.
Line a pan with foil to make a packet for the Tilapia, carrots and apples.

In a juicer, make fresh apple juice from two Granny Smith apples.
Thinly slice the remaining two Granny Smith apples.
Spread carrots on the bottom of the foil-lined pan.
Rinse the Tilapia and pat dry with paper towels.
Using a brush, coat both sides of the filet with the fresh apple juice.
Place the filet on top of the carrots.
Cover the Tilapia with the apple slices.
Fold the foil to create the packet.
Bake at 450F for 25-30 minutes.
Serve warm.

Tip: Instead of apple juice you can brush the Tilapia with fish stock (see recipe, p. 79).
Serving suggestion: Add fresh parsley on top.

Nutrition facts:
Portions: 2
Amount per portion:

Calories 380	Fat Cal. 60	**Total Fat** 6g (10%DV)
Sat. Fat 2g (11%DV)	*Trans* Fat 0g	**Cholest.** 130mg (43%DV)
Sodium 170mg (7%DV)	**Total carb.** 24g (8%DV)	Fiber 5g (20%DV)
Sugars 17g	**Protein** 60g	Vitamin A (160%DV)
Vitamin C (15%DV)	Calcium (6%DV)	Iron (10%DV)

Percent Daily Values (DV) are based on a 2,000 calorie diet.

BROILED TILAPIA OR FLOUNDER FILET

Ingredients for 2 portions:

---

1 lb (454g) Tilapia filet

Note: The recipe is the same for Tilapia or Flounder filet, but I have provided the nutrition facts separately.

Rinse the Tilapia and pat dry with paper towels.
Create a foil packet for the Tilapia—if you are making two portions, the packet will need to be slightly larger.
Bake on the middle shelf at 450F for 10 minutes on a baking stone or directly on the oven rungs.
Remove the Tilapia from the packet and flip it over, using a wide spatula.
Bake for another 7 minutes.
While the Tilapia is baking, switch to the broiler and broil for additional 3 minutes or until the Tilapia is golden. Serve warm in the foil.

TIP: Serving suggestions: Top with freshly juiced Granny Smith apples, or a few drops of fresh lemon juice, or add a thinly sliced Granny Smith apple to the fish. You could also serve with minced parsley and cooked, sliced carrots.

Nutrition facts for Tilapia:
Portions: 2
Amount per portion:

Calories 290	Fat Cal. 50	**Total Fat** 6g (9%DV)
Sat. Fat 2g (11%DV)	*Trans* Fat 0g	**Cholest.** 130mg (43%DV)
Sodium 125mg (5%DV)	**Total carb.** 0g (0%DV)	Fiber 0g (0%DV)
Sugars 0g	**Protein** 59g	Vitamin A (0%DV)
Vitamin C (0%DV)	Calcium (4%DV)	Iron (8%DV)

For Flounder:

Calories 270	Fat Cal. 30	**Total Fat** 3.5g (5%DV)
Sat. Fat 1g (4%DV)	*Trans* Fat 0g	**Cholest.** 155mg (51%DV)
Sodium 240mg (10%DV)	**Total carb.** 0g (0%DV)	Fiber 0g (0%DV)
Sugars 0g	**Protein** 55g	Vitamin A (2%DV)
Vitamin C (0%DV)	Calcium (4%DV)	Iron (4%DV)

Percent Daily Values (DV) are based on a 2,000 calorie diet.

SEARED YELLOWFIN TUNA, ZUCCHINI & CARROTS

Ingredients for 4 portions:

3.5oz (100g) (1 small, with skin) Granny Smith apple
½ lb (227g) wild yellowfin tuna
17oz (482g) (2½ medium) zucchini
4oz (113g) (12 medium) baby carrots
½ tsp (0.11oz, 3g) sea salt
2 large eggs

Thinly slice the Granny Smith apples.
Rinse the tuna with water and pat dry with paper towels.
Create a foil packet for the tuna.
Line the packet with part of the apple slices.
Place the tuna on top of the apples.
Cover the tuna with the rest of the apple slices.
Fold up the packet.
Bake at 450F for 25 minutes. Take out of the oven, open the packet and let cool.
Dice the vegetables and mix in a mixing bowl.
Dice the tuna and add to the mix.
Add the salt to the eggs and add to the mix.
Cook in a non-stick casserole on medium heat while stirring with a wooden spoon until the zucchini is clear and tender.
Serve warm.

Tip: Top with freshly squeezed apple juice.

Nutrition facts:
Portions: 4
Amount per portion:

Calories 160	Fat Cal. 30	**Total Fat** 3.5g (6%DV)
Sat. Fat 1g (5%DV)	*Trans* Fat 0g	**Cholest.** 140mg (46%DV)
Sodium 400mg (16%DV)	**Total carb.** 10g (3%DV)	Fiber 3g (10%DV)
Sugars 7g	**Protein** 22g	Vitamin A (90%DV)
Vitamin C (40%DV)	Calcium (6%DV)	Iron (10%DV)

Percent Daily Values (DV) are based on a 2,000 calorie diet

CHICKEN STOCK

2 ¼ lbs (1135g) chicken back & neck
3 cups (24fl oz, 710g) water
½ tsp (0.11oz, 3g) sea salt
2oz (60g) (2/3 cup) parsley
5oz (142g) (¾ medium) zucchini

Put all ingredients in a pot.
Bring to boil and simmer for 25 minutes.
Using a fine conical sieve or colander, filter the stock.
If not for an immediate use, let cool and refrigerate in a tightly closed container.

Note: The nutrition facts for this particular chicken stock are not available in the USDA tables or the Nutra Coster software. I used what I considered to be the closest stock, which in the USDA table is called "06172, soup, stock, chicken, home prepared" (http://ndb.nal.usda.gov/ndb/foods/show/1264). The following nutrition facts are for 1 cup (8.47 oz, 240 g) of this stock.

Calories 90	Fat Cal. 25	**Total Fat** 3g (4%DV)
Sat. Fat 1g (4%DV)	*Trans* Fat 0g	**Cholest.** 5mg (2%DV)
Sodium 340mg (14%DV)	**Total carb.** 8g (3%DV)	Fiber 0g (0%DV)
Sugars 4g	**Protein** 6g	Vitamin A (0%DV)
Vitamin C (0%DV)	Calcium (0%DV)	Iron (2%DV)

Percent Daily Values (DV) are based on a 2,000 calorie diet

BROILED CHICKEN BREAST

Ingredients for 2 portions:

---

1 lb (454g) chicken breast, thinly sliced
0.5 cup (4.23oz, 120g) chicken stock

If you purchase the chicken breast frozen, let it defrost for up to 24 hours in the refrigerator before using. Take the meat out of the refrigerator one hour before cooking.

Before broiling, marinate the chicken breast for 5 minutes in chicken stock.
Place the chicken on foil, and crimp the edges to prevent the juices from spilling into the pan.
Broil for 4 minutes on one side and 3 to 4 minutes on the other side. Do not overcook.
Take the chicken breast out of the broiler and cut a small slice on a cutting board to see if it is done (depending on whether you prefer it rare, medium rare, medium, or well-done).
Serve immediately.

Serving suggestions:
Serve with freshly squeezed Granny Smith apple juice.
Top with fresh parsley, a bit of fresh dill, and wrap in a light tortilla (see recipe, p. 56)

Tip: You can use beef stock instead of chicken stock.
You can sear in a grill pan (in photo below).

Nutrition facts:
Portions: 2
Amount per portion:

Calories 400	Fat Cal. 80	**Total Fat** 9g (14%DV)
Sat. Fat 2.5g (12%DV)	*Trans* Fat 0g	**Cholest.** 195mg (65%DV)
Sodium 250mg (11%DV)	**Total carb.** 2g (1%DV)	Fiber 0g (0%DV)
Sugars 1g	**Protein** 72g	Vitamin A (0%DV)
Vitamin C (0%DV)	Calcium (4%DV)	Iron (15%DV)

Percent Daily Values (DV) are based on a 2,000 calorie diet

BEEF BRISKET

Ingredients for 8 portions:

---

2 lbs (908g) beef brisket, first cut
2 lbs 2oz (964g) chicken stock, divided (see recipe p. 85)
1 lb 11oz (765g) (77 medium) baby carrots
4oz (113g) (14 uncooked) organic dried figs

Preparation:
If you purchase the brisket frozen, let it defrost for up to 24 hours in the refrigerator before using. Take it out of the refrigerator one hour before cooking.
Trim as much fat as possible from the brisket. Rinse and pat dry with paper towels.
Divide the chicken stock into three portions: 7 oz in one container, 20 oz in another, and 7 oz in a third.
Pour the 20 oz of stock into a glass or a ceramic dish that can be covered.
Quarter the dried figs.
Layer half the carrots and figs at the bottom of the dish.
Preheat the oven to 350F.
Preheat a heavy skillet, pour 7 oz of the stock into the skillet and brown the brisket on all sides.
Put the brisket in the Pyrex dish on the layer of carrots and figs.
Baste the brisket on all sides with the chicken stock that is in the pan.
Cover the top and the sides with the remaining carrots and figs.
Cook in the oven, covered, for 35 minutes, then remove.
Let the brisket cool for 5 minutes.
Transfer the brisket to a cutting board.
Using a long, straight carving knife, cut the brisket, across the grain, into ¼- inch thick slices.
Using a wide spatula, place the slices back in the Pyrex dish and cover again with the carrots and figs.
Cook for another 70 minutes at 350F and take out of the oven.
Using a spoon, baste the top and sides of the brisket with the stock that is in the Pyrex dish.
Cook for another 35 minutes at 350F and remove from the oven.
Check for tenderness.
The brisket should be melting in your mouth when ready.
Pour in the remaining 7 oz of chicken stock and baste all sides of the brisket.
If it is not yet fully cooked, bake for another 25 to 35 minutes at 350F, depending upon tenderness. Be careful not to burn the top and sides. Baste the top and sides with the chicken stock each time you take the brisket out of the oven.
Serve warm.
Enjoy! This is a wonderful treat!
Tip: Letting the meat defrost for 24 hours and then bringing it to room temperature are essential steps to make sure that the meat is tender.

BEEF STEAK

Ingredients for 8 portions:

---

3 lbs (1361g) prime beef sirloin steak
1 cup (8.47oz, 240g) beef stock

The deal is simple: good meat, thoroughly defrosted, good stock, and a careful broiling. If you purchase the beef frozen, let it defrost for up to 24 hours in the refrigerator before using. Take the beef out of the refrigerator one hour before cooking.

Before broiling, marinate the steak for 5 minutes in beef stock.
Line the pan with foil, crimping the edges to prevent the juices from spilling into the pan.
Broil for 4 minutes on each side.
Take the steak out of the broiler and cut a small slice on a cutting board to see if it is done (depending on whether you prefer it rare, medium rare, medium, or well-done).
Serve immediately.

Serving suggestions:
Served as is, a good beef steak is a celebration in itself.
Cut into small cubes and add to brown rice.
Cut into small cubes and add to a green salad.

Tip: You can use chicken stock instead of beef stock.

Nutrition facts:
Portions: 8
Amount per portion:

Calories 350	Fat Cal. 130	**Total Fat** 15g (23%DV)
Sat. Fat 6g (29%DV)	*Trans* Fat 0g	**Cholest.** 110mg (37%DV)
Sodium 170mg (7%DV)	**Total carb.** 0g (0%DV)	Fiber 0g (0%DV)
Sugars 0g	**Protein** 51g	Vitamin A (0%DV)
Vitamin C (0%DV)	Calcium (4%DV)	Iron (20%DV)

Percent Daily Values (DV) are based on a 2,000 calorie diet

BEEF STEW

Ingredients for 5 portions:

1½ lbs (680g) beef chuck
1 cup (8.47oz, 240g) beef stock, divided
½ tsp (0.11oz, 3g) sea salt

Preheat the oven to 350F.
Rinse the beef and pat dry with paper towels.
Add ½ cup of the beef stock and ½ tsp salt to a glass or ceramic pan with a lid.
Add the remaining ½ cup of the beef stock to a non-stick wok. The wok will be used to stir-fry the beef before baking it.
Heat the wok on high.
Stir-fry the beef on all sides until it changes color.
Transfer to the Pyrex pan and cover.
Cook in the oven at 350F for 45 minutes.
Remove the dish from the oven and stir the cubes, making sure the broth and juices are well-distributed.
Slice one of the cubes to check for tenderness.
Cover the pan and return it to the oven for another 20 minutes or until tender.

Tip: Add raw eggs still in the shell to the pan and cook with the beef. The broth will seep into the eggs and impart a wonderful flavor.

Serving suggestion: Serve with cooked vegetables: Microwave the thawed beef cubes until the fat melts. Add the vegetables to the pan, coating them with the beef juices.
Let the pan rest for an hour to let the beef juices seep into the vegetables and serve warm.

Nutrition facts:
Portions: 5
Amount per portion:

Calories 390 Fat	Cal. 210	**Total Fat** 24g (37%DV)
Sat. Fat 9g (47%DV)	*Trans* Fat 0g	**Cholest.** 120mg (40%DV)
Sodium 400mg (17%DV)	**Total carb.** 1g (0%DV)	Fiber 0g (0%DV)
Sugars 0g	**Protein** 41g	Vitamin A (0%DV)
Vitamin C (0%DV)	Calcium (2%DV)	Iron (20%DV)

Percent Daily Values (DV) are based on a 2,000 calorie diet

BEEF STOCK

1.5 lbs (680g) beef soup bones
2 cups (16fl oz, 474g) water
½ tsp sea salt
1.4oz (40g) (½ cup) parsley
3.5oz (100g) (10 medium) baby carrots
1.4oz (40g) (4 ½ cups, sprigs) dill

Put all ingredients together in a pot.
Bring to a boil and simmer for 45 minutes.
Using a fine conical sieve or colander, filter the stock.
If you are not using immediately, let cool and refrigerate in a tightly closed container.

Note: The nutrition facts for this particular beef stock are not available in the USDA tables or the Nutra Coster software. I used what I considered to be the closest stock, which in the USDA table is called "06170, Soup, stock, beef, home-prepared" (http://ndb.nal.usda.gov/ndb/foods/show/1263). The following nutrition facts are for 1 cup (8.47 oz, 240 g) of this stock.

Calories 30	Fat Cal. 0	**Total Fat** 0g (0%DV)
Sat. Fat 0g (0%DV)	*Trans* Fat 0g	**Cholest.** 0mg (0%DV)
Sodium 480mg (20%DV)	**Total carb.** 3g (1%DV)	Fiber 0g (0%DV)
Sugars 1g	**Protein** 5g	Vitamin A (0%DV)
Vitamin C (0%DV)	Calcium (2%DV)	Iron (4%DV)

Percent Daily Values (DV) are based on a 2,000 calorie diet

MEATLOAF

Ingredients for 8 portions:

1.5 lbs (680g) naturally-raised ground beef, sirloin
12oz (340g) bean sprouts
1oz (28g) (1/3 cup) parsley
½ tsp (0.11oz, 3g) sea salt
2 large eggs
½ cup, plus 1 tbsp polenta or medium ground cornmeal, divided

---

Finely chop the bean sprouts and parsley.
Add the salt to the eggs and mix all of the ingredients except for the ½ cup polenta in a mixing bowl.
Divide the ½ cup polenta among the cups of a muffin pan. You can also use a silicone pan for medium-size cupcakes or a loaf pan.
Divide the mixture into 8 portions, and place each portion into one of the cups of the muffin tin.
Bake at 350F for 30 minutes and then raise the temperature to 450F and cook for 10 minutes.
Serve warm.

Tip: The first 30 minutes are for cooking the meat and the next 10 minutes are for removing excess moisture and providing color. You can vary the cooking time at 450F from 5 to15 minutes, according to how moist you prefer the loaves.

Nutrition facts:
Portions: 8
Amount per portion:

Calories 280	Fat Cal. 90	**Total Fat** 10g (16%DV),
Sat. Fat 4g (19%DV)	*Trans* Fat 0.5g	**Cholest.** 110mg (36%DV),
Sodium 230mg (10%DV)	**Total carb.** 22g (7%DV)	Fiber 0g (0%DV),
Sugars 0g	**Protein** 23g	Vitamin A (8%DV),
Vitamin C (35%DV)	Calcium (2%DV)	Iron (20%DV)

Percent Daily Values (DV) are based on a 2,000 calorie diet

HAMBURGER

Ingredients for 4 portions:

1oz (28g) (1/3 cup) parsley
1 lb (454g) naturally-raised ground beef, sirloin
½ tsp (0.11oz, 3g) sea salt
2 large eggs

Finely chop the parsley.
Add salt to eggs.
Mix all of the ingredients in a mixing bowl.
Divide into four sections and form patties.
Put the patties on foil in a flat pan or a skillet.
Broil each side for 3 minutes.

Tip: Serve with a sprig of fresh parsley. If you are missing the wheat buns, try making a wrap with a light tortilla (see recipe p. 56).

Nutrition facts:
Portion : 4
Amount per portion:

Calories 280	Fat Cal. 140	**Total Fat** 16g (24%DV)
Sat. Fat 6g (30%DV)	*Trans* Fat 1g	**Cholest.** 200mg (67%DV)
Sodium 420mg (17%DV)	**Total carb.** 1g (0%DV)	Fiber 0g (0%DV)
Sugars 0g	**Protein** 33g	Vitamin A (15%DV)
Vitamin C (15%DV)	Calcium (4%DV)	Iron (20%DV)

Percent Daily Values (DV) are based on a 2,000 calorie diet

SIDE DISHES

Opposite page: Yam and Sweet Potato Chips, p. 106

BAKED ZUCCHINI

Rinse the zucchini.
Place the whole zucchini on parchment paper in a baking pan.
Bake at 450F for 25-30 minutes.
Cool.
Cut into ¼-inch thick slices.
Tip: Serve with freshly cut slices of avocado, slices of hard-boiled egg, or eggs sunny side up.

BAKED BROCCOLI

Rinse the broccoli.
Remove the stems, leaving only the florets.
Line a baking pan with parchment paper and layer the broccoli florets.
Bake at 450F for 25-30 minutes on the lower shelf until the broccoli is brown on top. Do not over-bake.

Tip: Serve with cooked chopped spinach and sunny side up eggs.

BAKED CAULIFLOWER

Rinse the cauliflower and remove the leaves.
Cut the cauliflower into ¼-inch slices.
Line a baking pan with parchment paper and layer the cauliflower slices.
Bake at 450F for 25-30 minutes on the lower shelf until the bottom of the cauliflower slices are brown.

Tip: Serve with fresh lettuce leaves, strips of freshly cut avocado, and dried edamame.

FOUR TYPES OF SQUASH

Note: The weights below are for the various squashes, baked and cleaned.

Ingredients:

8oz (227g) acorn squash (1 portion)
32oz (907g) butternut squash (4 portions)
14oz (397g) kabocha squash (2 portions)
33oz (936g) spaghetti squash (4 portions)

The following preparation pertains to the following four types of squash: acorn, butternut, kabocha, and spaghetti.

Squash of all types is a wonderful ingredient that provides varying tastes and textures. Peeling squash can be a challenge, so here is the easy way to prepare a squash.

Heat the oven to 450F.
Rinse the squash.
Put on a parchment paper.
You can fully bake at 450F for 40-45 minutes, or you can partially bake for 30 minutes, at which point you can easily peel off the skin.
Let cool.
Peel off the skin, either with your hands or with a knife.
Cut open and remove the seeds.
Store in a closed container in the refrigerator.

BAKED CORN ON THE COB

Corn on the cob can be prepared in many ways: you can boil it, grill it, or sear it. But my favorite way is the one of the simplest and the results are great!

Preheat the oven to 450F. Check each ear and remove any outer leaves that could stick out and catch fire in the oven. To prevent burning, trim the leaves and the silk but make sure the corn is covered and the kernels are not exposed.
Holding the ear vertically under the faucet, saturate the leaves, to prevent burning.
Arrange the ears on a parchment-lined baking sheet or directly on the oven rungs and bake for 15 minutes.
Take the sheet out of the oven, and using rubber gloves, run the ears under the faucet once again.
Put the corn back on the baking sheet with the baked side up, and bake for another 15 minutes at 450F.
Remove the ears, let them cool, and then husk them. Serve warm.

Tip: Keep the ears you have not yet husked in the refrigerator so they stay fresh.

EDAMAME IN THE POD

Ingredients:

½ tsp (0.11oz, 3g) sea salt
4 cups (32oz, 947g) water
12oz (340g) edamame in pods, frozen

Add salt to water and bring to boil.
Add frozen edamame and bring to boil.
Cook 11 minutes on medium heat.
Rinse and serve warm.

BAKED YAMS AND SWEET POTATOES

Ingredients for 1 portion:

8oz (230g) (1 2/3 cups, cubes, raw) yams
8oz (230g) (1 2/3 cups, cubes, raw) sweet potatoes
Note: The approximate quantities in cups are estimates only, so do not cut into cubes.

Baking with the peel still on:
Heat the oven to 450F.
Wash the yams and the sweet potatoes.
Place on baking paper in a pan.
Place in the oven and bake for 55-60 minutes.
Take out of the oven and let cool.
Peel and serve warm.

Tip: Mash the yams and sweet potatoes and serve with fresh avocado.

Baking without the peel:
Heat the oven to 450F.
Wash the yams and the sweet potatoes.
Peel the yams and sweet potatoes and cut in half on the vertical.
Place the yams and sweet potatoes separately on parchment paper in a pan and bake for 25 minutes on the bottom shelf.
Take out of the oven and let cool for 5 minutes.
Using a paring knife, make four slices along the tops of the yams and the sweet potatoes to score. This will make it easier to slice when the yams and potatoes are fully cooked.
Put back into oven on the middle shelf and bake the yams for another 15 minutes (for a total of 40 minutes) and the sweet potatoes for another 25 minutes (for a total of 50 minutes).
Serve warm.

Tip: Serve with either fresh avocado or natural unsweetened applesauce.

YAM AND SWEET POTATO CHIPS

Ingredients for 1 portion:

8oz (230g) (1 2/3 cups, cubes, raw) yams
8oz (230g) (1 2/3 cups, cubes, raw) sweet potatoes
Note: The approximate quantities in cups are estimates only, so do not cut into cubes.

This is a very simple and wonderful dish. Whenever I prepare the chips I have to make sure that I put them away after they cool. Otherwise, the gremlins will make them disappear.

Heat the oven to 450F.
Wash the yams and the sweet potatoes.
Cut both ends and peel away the skin.
Heat the oven to 450F.
Using either a mandolin or a knife, slice the yams and the sweet potatoes across into ¼-inch slices. You can also slice them lengthwise, but if you do, use a mandolin because it's safer.
Place the slices on parchment paper or on a baking grid or rack. Chips of yams or sweet potatoes usually fit on standard size baking paper or a silicone baking mat.

Note: Bake the yams and sweet potatoes on separate baking grids because yams have a higher water content so they need a longer baking time.
Place in the oven and bake for 15 minutes.
Take out of the oven and let cool 5 minutes or until you can handle the chips.
Turn the chips over and bake for another 10 or 15 minutes, being careful not to let them burn.
Let cool. Serve either warm or room temperature.

Tips:
Optional topping: Natural unsweetened applesauce.
If you refrigerate, it is best to do so in a container without a lid because a good refrigerator will dry out the chips.

BROWN RICE

Ingredients for 8 portions:

2 cups (14.50oz, 411g) brown rice
4 cups (32fl oz, 947g) water
½ tsp (0.11oz, 3g) sea salt

Bring water to boil.
Add rice and stir once.
Simmer 50 minutes, covered.
Let stand for 10 minutes.

WILD RICE

Ingredients for 4 portions:

½ tsp (0.11oz, 3g) sea salt
3 cups (24fl oz, 710g) water
1 cup (6.5oz, 185g) wild rice

Add salt to water and bring to boil.
Add wild rice and cook for 5 minutes.
Reduce heat to simmer and cook for another 45-50 minutes until the wild rice is tender.

DESSERTS

Opposite page: Dan's fruit salad, p. 108

DAN'S FRUIT SALAD

Ingredients for 2 portions:

8oz (230g) (2 medium, 7 to 7 7/8-inch long) bananas
7oz (200g) (1 medium) pear
7oz (200g) (3, 2-inch diameter) kiwis

Optional:
You can replace the pear with a 7 oz (200g) apple
You can make the following additions to the basic recipe:
0.3 oz (8 g) organic dried figs
0.25 oz (7 g) organic prunes
0.25 oz (7 g) blueberries and blackberries

Coarsely chop the fruit and combine. Serve immediately.

Nutrition facts:
Portions: 2
Amount per portion:

Calories 180	Fat Cal. 10	**Total Fat** 1g (1%DV)
Sat. Fat 0g (0%DV)	*Trans* Fat 0g	**Cholest.** 0mg (0%DV)
Sodium 0mg (0%DV)	**Total carb.** 45g (15%DV)	Fiber 8g (32%DV)
Sugars 27g	**Protein** 2g	Vitamin A (2%DV)
Vitamin C (110%DV)	Calcium (2%DV)	Iron (2%DV)

Percent Daily Values (DV) are based on a 2,000 calorie diet

PEAR SMOOTHIE

Ingredients for 3 portions:

7oz (200g) (1 medium) pear
3.50oz (100g) (1½, 2-inch diameter) kiwis
8.00oz (230g) (2 medium, 7 to 7 7/8-inch long) bananas
1.5 cup (12.90oz, 360g) unsweetened organic soy or almond milk

---

Peal the fruit and coarsely chop.
Process in a blender until smooth and serve immediately.

Tip: For a thicker smoothie, use only half as much soy milk.

Nutrition facts:
Portions: 3
Amount per portion:

Calories 150	Fat Cal. 20	**Total Fat** 2.5g (4%DV)
Sat. Fat 0g (0%DV)	*Trans* Fat 0g	**Cholest.** 0mg (0%DV)
Sodium 45mg (2%DV)	**Total carb.** 31g (10%DV)	Fiber 6g (22%DV)
Sugars 18g,	**Protein** 5g	Vitamin A (2%DV)
Vitamin C (70%DV)	Calcium (15%DV)	Iron (4%DV)

Percent Daily Values (DV) are based on a 2,000 calorie diet

APPLE SMOOTHIE

Ingredients for 3 portions:

8oz (225g) (2 medium, 7 to 7 7/8-inch long) bananas
7oz (200g) (1½ small, with skin) Granny Smith apples
3.5oz (100g) (1½, 2-inch diameter) kiwis
1.5 cups (12.90oz, 360g) unsweetened organic soy or almond milk

---

Peel the fruit and coarsely chop.
Process in a blender until smooth and serve immediately.

Tip: For a thicker smoothie, use only half as much soy milk.

Nutrition facts:
Portions: 3
Amount per portion:

Calories 170	Fat Cal. 20	**Total Fat** 2.5g (4%DV)
Sat. Fat 0g (0%DV)	*Trans* Fat 0g	**Cholest.** 0mg (0%DV)
Sodium 45mg (2%DV)	**Total carb.** 35g (12%DV)	Fiber 5g (20%DV)
Sugars 21g	**Protein** 5g	Vitamin A (2%DV)
Vitamin C (70%DV)	Calcium (15%DV)	Iron (6%DV)

Percent Daily Values (DV) are based on a 2,000 calorie diet

BAKED APPLES

Ingredients for 1 portion:

7oz (200g) (1½ small, with skin) Granny Smith apples
1oz (28g) (1) pitted Medjool date

Process:
Core a Granny Smith apple and combine with the pitted date.
Bake at 450F for 15 minutes in small heat-resistant glass bowl or ramekin.
Serve warm.

Tip: For topping, add prune juice.

Nutrition facts:
Portions: 1
Amount per portion:

Calories 170	Fat Cal. 0	**Total Fat** 0g (0%DV)
Sat. Fat 0g (0%DV)	*Trans* Fat 0g	**Cholest.** 0mg (0%DV)
Sodium 0mg (0%DV)	**Total carb.** 46g (15%DV)	Fiber 6g (26%DV)
Sugars 37g	**Protein** 1g	Vitamin A (2%DV)
Vitamin C (15%DV)	Calcium (2%DV)	Iron (2%DV)

Percent Daily Values (DV) are based on a 2,000 calorie diet

FRUIT COMPOTE

Ingredients for 3 portions:

7oz (200g) (1 medium) pear
7oz (200g) (1½ small) apples
2.50oz (70g) (3) Medjool dates, pitted
0.75oz (20g) (2, dried, uncooked, pitted) prunes, organic
1oz (30g) (4 dried, uncooked) figs, organic
0.5 cup (2.80oz, 80g) (5oz, 145g) seedless raisins
0.5 cup (4.60oz, 130g) organic grape juice

Coarsely chop the fruit.
Add grape juice.
Boil for five minutes, stirring occasionally. Make sure some liquid remains so the compote does not burn.
Let cool.

Tip: Serve by itself or as a topping for a pudding.

Nutrition facts:
Portions: 3
Amount per portion:

Calories 280	Fat Cal. 5	**Total Fat** 0.5g (1%DV)
Sat. Fat 0g (0%DV)	*Trans* Fat 0g	**Cholest.** 0mg (0%DV)
Sodium 5mg (0%DV)	**Total carb.** 74g (25%DV)	Fiber 8g (30%DV)
Sugars 54g	**Protein** 2g	Vitamin A (4%DV)
Vitamin C (10%DV)	Calcium (6%DV)	Iron (8%DV)

Percent Daily Values (DV) are based on a 2,000 calorie diet

GRITS PUDDING

Ingredients for 4 portions:

Pudding:
3 cups (25oz, 710g) water
½ cup (4.20oz, 120g) grape juice, organic
dash (0.01oz, 0.25g) sea salt
½ cup (3.90oz, 110g) white grits

Filling:
1.75oz (50g) dried figs, organic
1oz (30g) dried prunes, organic
1oz (30g) Medjool dates, pitted
7oz (20g) dried apples, organic, unsulfured
7oz (20g) dried apricots, organic, unsulfured

To make the filling:
Prepare the filling first.
Cut the dried fruit into medium-sized (½-inch) chunks and divide into four portions.
Put one- fourth in each of the containers (ramekin or pudding cup). In a later step, you are going to pour the warm grits over the fruit.

To make the pudding:
Boil the grape juice and water with the salt. Add the grits, reduce the heat to medium-low, and cook, stirring, for at least 5 minutes. Pour the grits into a bowl or measuring cup and then pour the mixture over the fruit. Mix the grits with the dried fruit and let cool. Cover and refrigerate. Serve either cold or warm.

Tip: For topping: Cut dried fruit into medium-sized (½-inch) chunks. Before serving, drizzle a bit of organic grape juice or organic prune juice over the pudding to add color and taste.

Nutrition facts:
Portions: 4
Amount per portion:

Calories 230	Fat Cal. 0	**Total Fat** 0.5g (1%DV)
Sat. Fat 0g (0%DV)	*Trans* Fat 0g	**Cholest.** 0mg (0%DV)
Sodium 50mg (2%DV)	**Total carb.** 53g (18%DV)	Fiber 2g (10%DV)
Sugars 20g	**Protein** 4g	Vitamin A (4%DV)
Vitamin C (2%DV)	Calcium (6%DV)	Iron (6%DV)

Percent Daily Values (DV) are based on a 2,000 calorie diet

FRUIT CUPCAKES

Ingredients for 20 medium-sized cupcakes:

8oz (230g) (2 medium, 7 to 7 7/8-inch long) bananas
7oz (200g) (1½ small, with skin) apples
7oz (200g) (1 medium) pear
3.5oz (100g) (1½ , 2-inch diameter) kiwis
3 large eggs
1 cup (5.30oz, 150g) fine corn flour

Chop the fruit in a food processor.
Using a mixer, beat the eggs with the whisk.
Switch to the paddle and mix all ingredients well.
Use a large scoop to place the batter in either a silicone cupcake pan
or regular cupcake pan with baking cup liners.
Bake at 425F for 25 minutes.

Tip: You can add one-half cup of berries for color and taste.
You can bake in a scone pan as well (see photo). Baking time is 25-30 minutes at 425F.

Nutrition facts:
Portions: 20
Amount per portion:

Calories 60	Fat Cal. 10	**Total Fat** 1g (2%DV)
Sat. Fat 0g (0%DV)	*Trans* Fat 0g	**Cholest.** 30mg (11%DV)
Sodium 10mg (0%DV)	**Total carb.** 12g (4%DV)	Fiber 1g (6%DV)
Sugars 4g	**Protein** 2g	Vitamin A (2%DV)
Vitamin C (10%DV)	Calcium (2%DV)	Iron (2%DV)

Percent Daily Values (DV) are based on a 2,000 calorie diet

BANANA BREAD

Ingredients for 12 portions:

---

3 large eggs
2.5 lbs (910g) (8¼ medium, 7 to 7 7/8-inch long) ripe bananas
7oz (200g) (1½ small, with skin) Granny Smith apples
2 cups (9.45oz, 270g) fine corn flour or polenta
½ cup (2.79oz, 79g) coarse cornmeal

Beat the whole eggs at high speed with the paddle.
Coarsely chop the bananas and apples into small cubes.
Add the bananas and apples to eggs and beat, gradually increasing the speed.
Add the fine corn flour (or polenta); start slowly and gradually increase the speed.
Dust two medium (8 x 4) loaf pans with the coarse cornmeal.
Add the batter and spread evenly.
Bake at 375F for 40 minutes on the lower shelf and then for 30 minutes on the middle shelf.
Let cool for 15 minutes in the pans.
Remove the loaf from the pan, turn it upside down, and let cool on a cooling rack.
After the loaf has cooled, scrape any residual cornmeal from the bottom.
Wrap up and refrigerate.

TIP: If you prefer a less pronounced banana flavor, reduce the bananas to 25 oz (710g) and add 7 oz (200g) finely chopped Bosc pears.

TIP: In the same vein, you can add organic dried prunes or figs (2 ¼ oz., 65 g) to add sweetness, flavor, and color. Finely chop before adding to the batter.

Nutrition Facts:
Portions: 12
Amount per portion:

Calories 200	Fat Cal. 20	**Total Fat** 2.5g (4%DV),
Sat. Fat 0.5g (3%DV)	*Trans* Fat 0g	**Cholest.** 55mg (18%DV)
Sodium 20mg (1%DV)	**Total carb** 41g (14%DV)	Fiber 4g (16%DV)
Sugars 12g	**Protein** 5g	Vitamin A (2%DV)
Vitamin C (15%DV)	Calcium (4%DV)	Iron (6%DV)

Percent Daily Values (DV) are based on a 2,000 calorie diet.

CARROT SMOOTHIE

Ingredients for 4 portions:

8oz (225g) (2 medium, 7 to 7 7/8-inch long) bananas
7oz (200g) (2 small, with skin) Granny Smith apples
7oz (200g) (1 medium) pear
2 cups (16.65oz, 470g) carrot juice

Peel the fruit and coarsely chop.
Juice the fresh carrots to get two cups of carrot juice.
Process in a blender until smooth and serve immediately.

Tip: For a thicker smoothie, use only half as much carrot juice.

Nutrition facts:
Portions: 4
Amount per portion:

Calories 140	Fat Cal. 0	**Total Fat** 0.5g (1%DV)
Sat. Fat 0g (0%DV)	*Trans* Fat 0g	**Cholest.** 0mg (0%DV)
Sodium 35mg (1%DV)	**Total carb.** 36g (12%DV)	Fiber 5g (22%DV)
Sugars 20g	**Protein** 2g	Vitamin A (450%DV)
Vitamin C (30%DV)	Calcium (4%DV)	Iron (4%DV)

Percent Daily Values (DV) are based on a 2,000 calorie diet

BIBLIOGRAPHY

Cooper, G. (2008). *The arthritis handbook: Improve your health and manage the pain of osteoarthritis.* New York, NY: DiaMedica Publishing.

Spiera, H, Kerr, L. D., & Yu, T. (1995). Nutrition and Arthritis. In V. Herbert & G.J. Subak Sharpe (Eds.), *Total nutrition: The only guide you'll ever need,* (pp. 599-61). New York, NY: St. Martin Press.

United States Department of Agriculture (n.d.). *Choose MyPlate.* Retrieved June 3rd, 2013 from http://www.choosemyplate.gov

United States Department of Agriculture & United States Department of Health and Human Services (2010). *Dietary Guidelines for Americans 2010 (7th ed.).* Washington, D.C.: U.S. Government Printing Office. Retrieved June 3rd, 2013 from http://www.health.gov/dietaryguidelines/dga2010/DietaryGuidelines2010.pdf.

United States Department of Agriculture (n.d.). *National Nutrient Database for Standard Reference.* Retrieved June 3rd, 2013 from http://ndb.nal.usda.gov/ndb/search/list.

SUGGESTED READING

Bittman, M. (2012). *How to cook everything. The basics: All you need to know to make great food.* Hoboken, New Jersey: John Wiley & Sons, Inc.

Culinary Institute of America, The (2009). *The professional chef (9th ed.).* Hoboken, New Jersey: John Wiley & Sons, Inc.

Pepin, J. (1987). *Jacques Pepin's the art of cooking* (Vol. 1). New York, NY: Alfred P. Knopf.

Pepin, J. (1988). *Jacques Pepin's the art of cooking* (Vol. 2). New York, NY: Alfred P. Knopf.

APPENDIX: DAN'S SAFE LIST

I would like to share *Dan's Safe List* as an example of a personal list; these are the ingredients I use in my own diet. I suggest that you develop your own *Safe List* with the assistance of a certified dietician and a doctor's supervision. I organized the list according to the five food groups in the USDA's *Choose MyPlate* (http://www.choosemyplate.gov).

Fruit:

Apples, avocado, bananas, kiwis, pears.

Vegetables:

Artichokes, broccoli, carrots, cauliflower, corn, cucumber, dill, parsley, lettuce, spinach, acorn squash, butternut squash, kabocha squash, spaghetti squash, sweet potatoes, yams, zucchini.

Grains:

Corn grits, polenta, corn meal (fine, medium and coarse), organic popcorn.

Protein:

Eggs, fish (flounder, tilapia), soy (dried edamame and frozen edamame in the pod).

Note: Because my intake of animal protein is limited, I supplement with vitamin B12.

Milk & Milk Products:

I do not include dairy products in my diet, so I supplement with calcium citrate plus vitamin D3.

INDEX

yellowfin tuna, zucchini and carrot, seared 84
Textured Vegetable Protein (TVP)
textured vegetable protein (TVP) and zucchini 48

V

variety in cooking 18
vegetable
vegetable soup 33

W

wild rice: see rice, wild
wild sardines: see sardines, wild

Y

yam
yam soup 36
yam and sweet potato, baked 104
yam and sweet potato chips 106
yams and sweet potatoes 49
yams and sweet potato patties 51
yam and sweet potato green salad 27
yams and sweet potatoes quiche 67
yams, sweet potatoes and zucchini, seared 50
yams, zucchini and apples, cooked 42
zucchini and yam quiche 64
yellowfin tuna: see tuna, yellowfin

Z

zucchini
tuna and zucchini omelet 77
textured vegetable protein (TVP) and zucchini 48
yellowfin tuna, zucchini and carrot, seared 84
yams, sweet potatoes and zucchini, seared 50
yams, zucchini and apples, cooked 42
zucchini and carrot quiche 62
zucchini and yams quiche 64
zucchini, avocado and spinach 44
zucchini, baked 100
zucchini, carrot and brown rice 45
zucchini, carrots, and two kinds of rice 46
zucchini, seared, and avocado 43

For questions: please email dan@bakerdan.com and visit www.bakerdan.com.